PRIMARY

C000228771

Art

6592UK

Dianne Sterrett

PRIMARY ART (Book G)

Published by R.I.C. Publications® 2007

Reprinted under licence by
Prim-Ed Publishing 2007

Copyright© Dianne Sterrett 2007

ISBN 978-1-84654-134-6

PR–6592

Additional titles available in this series:
PRIMARY ART (Book A)
PRIMARY ART (Book B)
PRIMARY ART (Book C)
PRIMARY ART (Book D)
PRIMARY ART (Book E)
PRIMARY ART (Book F)

Distributed by

AUSTRALIA: **R.I.C. Publications®**
PO Box 332, Greenwood WA 6924

UK: **Prim-Ed Publishing**
PO Box 2840, Coventry CV6 5ZY

IRELAND: **Prim-Ed Publishing**
Bosheen, New Ross, Co. Wexford

This master may only be reproduced by the
original purchaser for use with their class(es). The
publisher prohibits the loaning or onselling of this
master for the purposes of reproduction.

Copyright Notice

Blackline masters or copy masters are published and
sold with a limited copyright. This copyright allows
publishers to provide teachers and schools with a
wide range of learning activities without copyright
being breached. This limited copyright allows the
purchaser to make sufficient copies for use within
their own education institution. The copyright is not
transferable, nor can it be onsold. Following these
instructions is not essential but will ensure that you,
as the purchaser, have evidence of legal ownership
to the copyright if inspection occurs.

For your added protection in the case of copyright
inspection, please complete the form below. Retain
this form, the complete original document and the
invoice or receipt as proof of purchase.

Name of Purchaser:

_____

Date of Purchase:

_____

Supplier:

_____

School Order# (if applicable):

_____

Signature of Purchaser:

_____

Offices in: United Kingdom: PO Box 2840, Coventry, CV6 5ZY   **Email:** sales@prim-ed.com
Australia: PO Box 332, Greenwood, Western Australia, 6924   **Email:** mail@ricgroup.com.au
Republic of Ireland: Bosheen, New Ross, Co. Wexford, Ireland   **Email:** sales@prim-ed.com
R.I.C. Asia: 5th Floor, Gotanda Mikado Building, 2–5–8 Hiratsuka,
Shinagawa-Ku Tokyo, Japan 142–0051   **Email:** elt@ricpublications.com

Internet websites

In some cases, websites or specific URLs may be recommended. While these are checked and rechecked at the
time of publication, the publisher has no control over any subsequent changes which may be made to webpages.
It is *strongly* recommended that the class teacher checks *all* URLs before allowing pupils to access them.

Website: www.ricgroup.com   www.prim-ed.com

Email: mail@ricgroup.com.au   sales@prim-ed.com

PRIMARY ART
Book G

Foreword

Primary art is a series of seven books designed to provide teachers with a collection of skills, ideas and techniques to support current curriculum requirements in the visual arts learning areas.

Titles in this series include:

- *Primary art – Book A*
- *Primary art – Book B*
- *Primary art – Book C*
- *Primary art – Book D*
- *Primary art – Book E*
- *Primary art – Book F*
- *Primary art – Book G*

Contents

Contents i

Teachers notes .... ii – v

The colour wheel vi

The colour wheel glossary vii

Art projects

1. Oil pastel/Wax resist bunch of flowers 2–5
2. Corrugated card flower greeting card 6–9
3. Metallic strip greeting card 10–13
4. Etched name leaning board 14–17
5. Metallic space scene 18–21
6. Repetitive drawing sea animal collage 22–25
7. Summer fabric design 26–29
8. Slipping and sliding 30–33
9. Porthole scene 34–37
10. Across the street 38–41
11. Chalk pastels star collage 42–45
12. Butterfly farm 46–49
13. Arbitrary printing 50–53
14. Corrugated card tropical fish 54–57
15. Terracotta hessian sacks 58–61
16. Me: A star 62–65
17. Mystical mermaid/merman 66–69
18. Summer bushfires 70–73

19. Terrific tourist T-shirt 74–77
20. Torn paper 'sun and sea' 78–81
21. City reflections 82–85
22. Spiral eye teaser 86–89
23. Sad clown contour drawing 90–93
24. White silhouette 94–97
25. Watercolour masterpiece 98–101
26. CD cover 102–105
27. Ceramic tile design 106–109
28. Word designs 110–113
29. Pencil mania collage 114–117
30. Simple self-portrait 118–121
31. Colourful creatures 122–125
32. Summer sunset 126–129

Resources

Resource index 130
1. Etched name leaning board 131
2. Porthole scene 132
3. Butterfly farm 133
4. Mermaid/Merman 134
5. Terrific tourist T-shirt 135
6. Ceramic tile design 136

R.I.C. Publications/Prim-Ed Publishing

Teachers notes

From the teacher

The activities within *Primary art* Books A–G, will provide teachers with a series of multiskilled, visual arts lessons and activities for a whole range of topics, themes and special events.

Covering all primary year levels, the series equips the busy classroom teacher with a range of lessons from the 'quick and easy' to the more sophisticated carrier projects that work over three to four lessons.

Each art project is accompanied by easy to use reflection and assessment record sheets, enabling the collection of relevant evidence to record student progress.

The reflection sheets provide a thoughtful evaluation of the student's own performance for each facet of the lesson.

Task assessment sheets provide a quick means to identify and record a student's performance in criteria which assess the given objectives.

Within the series, students are given the opportunity to dabble with different media and to experience and build on a broad spectrum of techniques and skills, creating effects that will enhance their artistic work.

As the students build on their repertoire of skills, ideas and arts knowledge, they begin to plan and create a desired look or effect through experimentation. It is important to understand that the finished product will vary in quality according to the level of skill development.

As experience builds, so does the ability of students to use their artwork for purposes other than just the thrill of being creative. Their work becomes meaningful, with a purpose in society.

Dianne Sterret

Art project activities

Art doesn't have to have high preparation requirements if basic supplies are kept well stocked. This can be achieved by enlisting an adult to collect and prepare materials.

Lessons throughout the series have been coded to identify the objectives addressed or to indicate the effective use:

● **Arts ideas:** *Creates artworks to express ideas.*

● **Arts skills and processes:** *Uses a range of visual arts skills, techniques, procedures, practices and technologies.*

○ **Arts responses:** *Uses an aesthetic understanding to acknowledge, reflect on and assess the arts.*

○ **Arts in society:** *Demonstrates an understanding of the part that the arts play in society.*

★ *Enlist adult help to assist with the preparation of tasks, to help children in managing various tasks, or to mount work or add finishing touches to projects where adult skills are required.*

More able students may be able to complete for themselves activities designated as requiring parent or adult helpers. Mounting artworks is dependent on the availability of that resource. For that reason, this step—which relates to many of the artworks—is optional, except where required for support or where part of the artwork is displayed offset, for special effect.

R.I.C. Publications/Prim-Ed Publishing

Teachers notes

Making life easy!

Setting up

Setting up a good resource base is essential for an effective art scheme of work, as having appropriate tools and materials at your fingertips takes the headache out of lesson preparation. Labelled empty photocopy paper boxes in a central location are very functional. Stack them neatly along a wall. Enlist adult help to set up and maintain your resources.

Basic school supplies

- acrylic paint – standard colours and fluorescent
- Edicol™ or vegetable dye
- brushes – small, medium and large
    – glue brushes
- cartridge paper – large, approx. 56 cm x 36 cm
    – medium A3
- litho paper – A4
    – large, approx. 56 cm x 36 cm
    – medium A3
- coloured card for mounting work (including black)
- coloured paper squares – glossy, matt and fluorescent
- tissue paper
- crepe paper
- string
- glitter – variety of colours

- pipe-cleaners – sparkly
- feathers
- lead pencils/erasers
- glue sticks
- coloured pencils
- wax crayons
- oil pastels (standard and fluorescent)
- thick black markers (e.g. Artline™ 70)
- fine black markers (e.g. Artline™ 200)
- scissors
- A3 portfolio (optional)
- craft glue 250 mL
- watercolour pencils
- coloured permanent markers
- hot glue guns

Useful collectables

- polystyrene trays to use as paint trays
- newspapers
- sponge blocks (offcuts available from foam rubber outlets)
- fabric scraps (students who do dancing often have an abundance of interesting fabric scraps at home)
- cardboard offcuts
- corks
- cereal boxes (both ends opened, then flattened for easy storage)
- utensils – spoons, forks, blunt kitchen knives, whisks
- ice-cream containers
- takeaway food containers
- clay (e.g. Northcote™ terracotta is very child-friendly)
- craft sticks
- masking tape
- strawboard or thick cardboard
- toothpicks
- foil
- plastic sheeting
- overhead transparencies

- liquid detergent
- mineral turpentine (low-smell substitutes are also available)
- hot glue gun and glue sticks
- wool (variety of colours)
- paper cutter
- staplers
- fishing line
- steel wool
- washing up sponges
- egg cartons
- biscuit cutters
- greeting cards
- Easter egg wrappers
- fur offcuts (pref. 'faux' fur)
- bubble wrap
- plastic bottle tops
- birthday wrapping paper
- curling ribbon
- paint samples

R.I.C. Publications/Prim-Ed Publishing

Teachers notes

Each art project is presented over four pages:

- teachers page
- full-colour photograph of completed art project
- student's reflection page
- task assessment

Teachers page

Art project title

Number of **lessons** included in the art project.

Colour **codes** identify **visual arts objectives** addressed in lesson activities (see page ii).

Key focus points to promote **discussion** of theme and for effective **lesson preparation**.

Simple, multiskilled **art activities** with effective results.

Project theme synopsis

Star code to indicate adult help.

Material requirements appropriate to each lesson. Activities make use of easily accessible resources/ mediums.

Butterfly farm

This activity was inspired by the theme *Insects* with a focus on 'butterflies'. A combination of 2-D and 3-D creates a realistic illusion of butterflies on a leafy background. Butterflies are attracted to colourful plants and flowers and this characteristic leads into the themes of colour and seasons. The maths concept of *symmetry* is also incorporated in this project.

Three-lesson project

Discussion points

A poster of the colour wheel showing primary, secondary and tertiary colours will inspire meaningful discussion.

- In which season of the year do most flowers bloom? (spring)
- What mini beasts live in the garden? (List these on the board.)
- What is an insect? Discuss characteristics: arthropod with three distinct body parts—head, thorax and abdomen; three pairs of legs; and usually wings. Which mini beasts are insects? (ants, beetles, bees, butterflies etc.)
- Butterflies flutter around the garden. What have you noticed about their wings? (They are the same on both sides—symmetrical. They are brightly coloured etc.)
- Why do you think butterflies are brightly coloured? (to camouflage themselves among the plants/flowers etc.)
- What are butterflies helping to do as they flutter from one flower to the next? (They transfer pollen, helping plants to pollinate and produce seeds for new plants.)
- What colours are butterflies? (all colours of the spectrum)
- Why do you think most people like butterflies? (They are colourful and beautiful to look at. They also help to keep our plants multiplying.)
- How could we encourage butterflies to come to our garden? (Plant lots of plants with colourful flowers; water regularly to create a damp environment etc.)
- What is a butterfly farm? (an enclosure where an environment/habitat has been created for the comfort and breeding of butterflies; usually open to the public in a similar fashion to the zoo)
- Which colours are warm colours? (red, orange, yellow, tan etc.)

Lesson one

Materials

- A4 cartridge paper (3 sheets per student)
- oil pastels (fluorescent colours if available)
- Edicol™ dye (sky blue)
- ★ prepared butterfly template (optional) (page 133)
- ★ recycled cardboard (approximately 9 cm x 9 cm)
- paintbrush (medium)
- scissors
- lead pencil
- newspaper to protect workspace
- card for mounting
- craft glue for mounting

Method

1. Following discussion, students use light green oil pastel to draw three leaves spaced around one sheet of A4 cartridge paper. (Emphasise strong, solid lines.) To create a realistic colour, draw and colour leaf centres with dark green oil pastel and smudge gently from centre outwards.
2. Paint remaining background with blue dye. Set aside to dry.
3. Repeat drawing and colouring of three leaves on second A4 sheet of cartridge paper.
4. Students draw their own butterfly shapes on recycled cardboard or use a photocopy of the butterfly shape (p. 133) to make a template.
5. Cut out butterfly shape.
6. Using lead pencil, students trace butterfly onto remaining sheet of A4 cartridge paper five times. (Odd numbers are always more aesthetically pleasing.)
7. Using warm colours (yellow, orange and red) and strong, solid colouring, colour butterfly wings using oil pastels with a back and forth line colouring technique to form stripes of colour. Vary the order of colours on each butterfly (as shown in example). Gently blend colours by smudging from the centre outwards.

★ 8. Enlist adult help to mount background onto coloured card before Lesson two.

Lesson two

Materials

- artwork in progress
- oil pastels (fluorescent if available)
- scissors
- hot glue guns or glue stick
- fine permanent black marker
- newspaper to protect workspace

Method

1. Complete colouring butterflies if unfinished.
2. Cut out butterflies and leaves on undyed page.
3. Using hot glue gun or glue stick generously, glue leaves into position on background, gently bending them to create a 3-D effect. (Glue gun provides a more durable result.) Set aside to dry.
4. Draw body detail using fine permanent black marker. (Remaining detail may be completed when butterfly has been glued onto background.)
5. Fold butterflies in half, position and glue them onto background using hot glue or glue stick generously.
6. Draw continuation of body and antennae using fine permanent black marker. Set aside to dry.

Lesson three

Materials

- reflection and assessment photocopies
- lead pencil
- coloured pencils

Method

1. Students complete reflection activity.
2. Teacher completes assessment record.

R.I.C. Publications/Prim-Ed Publishing

Completed art project

Art project title

Butterfly farm

R.I.C. Publications/Prim-Ed Publishing

Clear, full-colour **photograph** of completed art project.

Teachers notes

Student reflection sheet

Related **art project title**

Objective and meaningful lesson **reflections**. Each provides a **self-analysis** of a student's **performance** for each key lesson point.

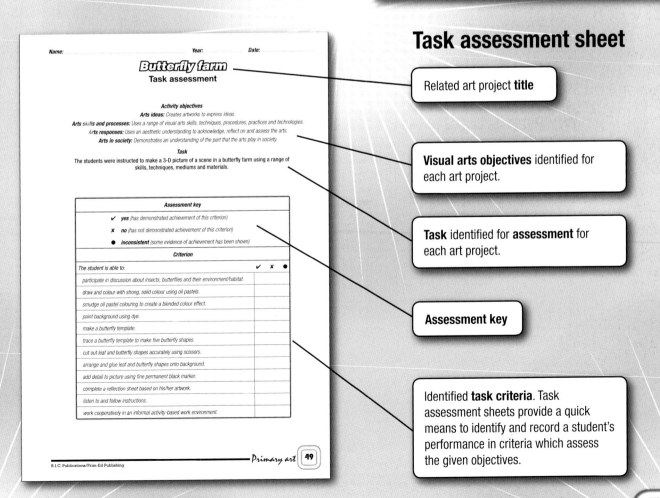

Butterfly farm
Reflections

1. List the characteristics of an insect. (Include the three body parts.)

2. Which part of this activity did you enjoy most? Give a reason for your answer.

3. List three techniques you used to create your Butterfly farm picture.

4. Would younger children find this art project difficult? Yes / No
   Give a reason for your answer.

5. Butterfly farms provide a comfortable environment/habitat for the butterflies to live in and breed. Draw/Design a butterfly enclosure, including three things which would ensure the butterflies live comfortably and safely. Label these. Colour your drawing with pencils.

48 *Primary art*   R.I.C. Publications/Prim-Ed Publishing

Task assessment sheet

Name: _____ Year: _____ Date: _____

Butterfly farm
Task assessment

Activity objectives
Arts ideas: *Creates artworks to express ideas.*
Arts skills and processes: *Uses a range of visual arts skills, techniques, procedures, practices and technologies.*
Arts responses: *Uses an aesthetic understanding to acknowledge, reflect on and assess the arts.*
Arts in society: *Demonstrates an understanding of the part that the arts play in society.*

Task
The students were instructed to make a 3-D picture of a scene in a butterfly farm using a range of skills, techniques, mediums and materials.

Assessment key			
✔	**yes** *(has demonstrated achievement of this criterion)*		
✗	**no** *(has not demonstrated achievement of this criterion)*		
●	**inconsistent** *(some evidence of achievement has been shown)*		

Criterion	✔	✗	●
The student is able to:			
participate in discussion about insects, butterflies and their environment/habitat.			
draw and colour with strong, solid colour using oil pastels.			
smudge oil pastel colouring to create a blended colour effect.			
paint background using dye.			
make a butterfly template.			
trace a butterfly template to make five butterfly shapes.			
cut out leaf and butterfly shapes accurately using scissors.			
arrange and glue leaf and butterfly shapes onto background.			
add detail to picture using fine permanent black marker.			
complete a reflection sheet based on his/her artwork.			
listen to and follow instructions.			
work cooperatively in an informal activity-based work environment.			

R.I.C. Publications/Prim-Ed Publishing   *Primary art* 49

Related art project **title**

Visual arts objectives identified for each art project.

Task identified for **assessment** for each art project.

Assessment key

Identified **task criteria**. Task assessment sheets provide a quick means to identify and record a student's performance in criteria which assess the given objectives.

Primary art ▼

The colour wheel

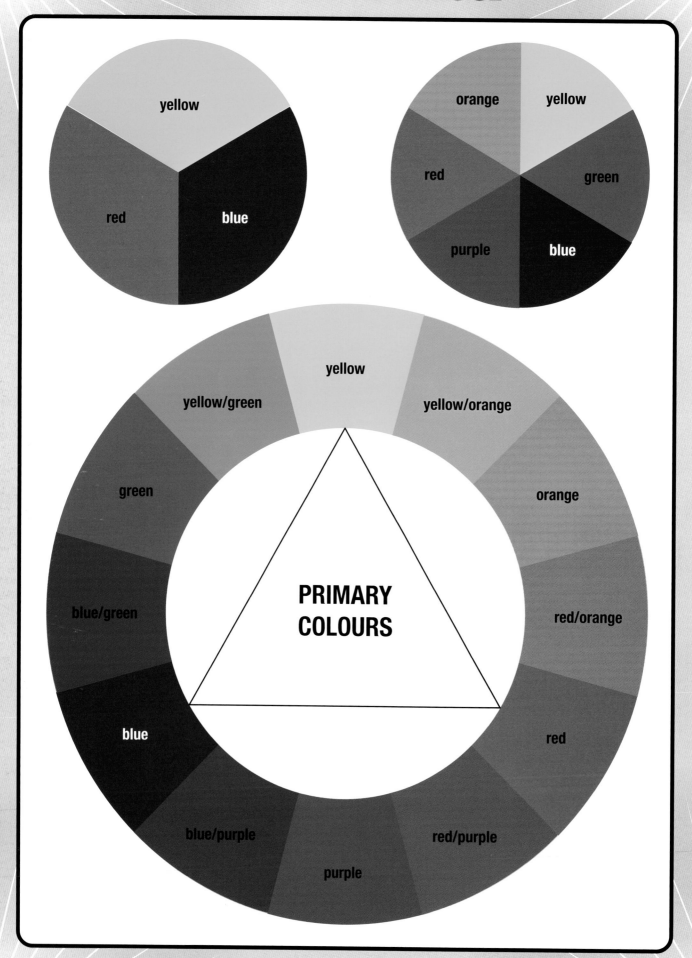

R.I.C. Publications/Prim-Ed Publishing

The colour wheel glossary

Hues

Variety of colours.

Primary colours

red, yellow and **blue**

These colours may be blended/mixed to make all other colours besides white and black.

Secondary colours

orange, green and **purple**

These colours are created when two primary colours are blended/mixed.

red + yellow = orange

yellow + blue = green

blue + red = purple

Intermediate colours

These colours are created by mixing one primary and one secondary colour.

red–orange

yellow–orange

yellow–green

blue–green

blue–purple

red–purple

Tertiary colours

These colours do not appear on the colour wheel and are created when any three primary colours are blended/mixed together in varying quantities.

Neutrals

White, black and **grey** (White for tints and black for shades.)

Tints

Tinting is a process where white is added to a base colour. Colours created are generally known as pastel colours. Large quantities of white are required to change a colour significantly.

Shades

Shades are created by adding black to a base colour. Only small amounts of black are required to make a base colour darker.

Complementary colours

These colours are opposites on the colour wheel. They are a strong contrast and stand out when adjacent to each other.

R.I.C. Publications/Prim-Ed Publishing

Oil pastel/Wax resist bunch of flowers

Flowers can be related to a wide range of themes; e.g. celebrations, seasons, gardens. The example shown was made as a gift for Mother's Day.

Two-lesson project

Discussion points

Pictures or photos of flowers will help to inspire meaningful discussion.

- In what season do most flowers bloom? (spring)
- What colours have you noticed in flower blossoms? (all colours of the spectrum)
- What features do flowering plants have? (petals, stamens, leaves, stems)
- Do petals have colour variations? (Many varieties of flowering plants have colour variations.)
- Where do most plants with flowers grow? (in sunny places)
- What flowers have you noticed in gardens? (roses, petunias, pansies, poppies, daisies etc.)

Some flowers grow directly from seeds, others from bulbs. (Many spring annuals grow from bulbs. These include tulips, daffodils, crocuses, among others.)

- What is it about flowers people like? (Their beauty, scent, bright and colourful, they attract insects and birds etc.)
- What do we use flowers for and why? (add colour to enhance our surroundings, enjoy in the garden, as gifts)
- Why do we cut flowers? (to admire flowers in places other than gardens etc.)
- Where do we put them to admire? (to decorate homes, workplaces, places of celebration, for weddings, funerals etc.)
- Who likes to receive flowers as a gift? (Mum, Nana, Grandma, Aunty etc.)
- Flowers are given as gifts for many reasons. What are some of the reasons we give gifts of appreciation? (to say we love someone, to say thank you, to say congratulations, to celebrate an occasion; e.g. birthday)

Lesson one

Materials

- A3 cartridge paper
- wax crayons or oil pastels
- Edicol™ dye (primary colours)
- paintbrush (medium)
- newspaper to protect workspace
- craft glue for mounting
- card for mounting

Note: Where several glue types are listed, hot glue is the most effective, however, other glue types will suffice.

Method

1. Following discussion about flowering plants and their components, teacher demonstrates how to draw a variety of line-drawn blooms to inspire students to design their own. See example. (Emphasise strong, solid colour.)
2. Students draw five or more flowers on top two-thirds of A3 paper using wax crayons or oil pastels. Instruct students to use at least two different flower designs.
3. Draw stems and leaves with green wax crayon or oil pastel.
4. Using dye, paint around flowers and stems. Set aside to dry.
★ 5. Enlist adult help to mount work onto coloured card.

Lesson two

Materials

- artwork in progress
★ - ribbon (approx. 65 cm per child, smaller lengths for smaller pictures)
- craft glue 250 mL (squeeze bottle)/hot glue gun
- reflection and assessment sheet photocopies
- lead pencil
- coloured pencils

Method

1. Tie ribbon into a bow.
2. Apply small blob of craft glue to bunch of stems.
3. Press bow into position. Apply pressure by placing a heavy book on top. Set aside to dry. (Alternatively, use a hot glue gun.)
4. Students complete reflection activity.
5. Teacher completes assessment record.

R.I.C. Publications/Prim-Ed Publishing

Oil pastel/Wax resist bunch of flowers

Oil pastel/Wax resist bunch of flowers
Reflections

1. Which mediums did you use to create a resist for the dye background?

   _____

2. What was necessary in your colouring technique to make sure the resist worked?

   _____

3. What did you enjoy most about this art activity? Give a reason for your answer.

   _____

   _____

   _____

4. List three ways this art project could be used; e.g. for a calendar.

   _____   _____   _____

5. Draw three different flower designs you could include in this activity. Colour your flower designs with pencils.

6. Flowers are often used to decorate giftware and household items. Draw and colour three items that could use our art project design to enhance their appearance.

R.I.C. Publications/Prim-Ed Publishing

Oil pastel/Wax resist bunch of flowers
Task assessment

Activity objectives

Arts ideas: *Creates artworks to express ideas.*

Arts skills and processes: *Uses a range of visual arts skills, techniques, procedures, practices and technologies.*

Arts responses: *Uses an aesthetic understanding to acknowledge, reflect on and assess the arts.*

Arts in society: *Demonstrates an understanding of the part that the arts play in society.*

Task

The students were instructed to make an oil pastel/wax resist picture using a range of skills, techniques, mediums and materials.

Assessment key			
✔ **yes** (has demonstrated achievement of this criterion)			
✗ **no** (has not demonstrated achievement of this criterion)			
● **inconsistent** (some evidence of achievement has been shown)			
Criterion			
The student is able to:	✔	✗	●
participate in discussion about seasons and flowers.			
design flowers for artwork.			
colour using strong, solid colour with wax crayons/oil pastels.			
add leaves and stems using wax crayons or oil pastels.			
paint background with dye.			
tie and attach bow to flowers.			
complete a reflection sheet based on his/her artwork.			
listen to and follow instructions.			
work cooperatively in an informal, activity-based work environment.			

Corrugated card flower greeting card

This card is simple and effective and may be used for any occasion; e.g. Mothers Day, birthday, thank you, get well etc.

Two-lesson project

Discussion points ●○○

Flowers can be related to a wide range of themes; e.g. celebrations, seasons, insects.

- What sort of things can you buy in a florist shop? (cut flowers such as roses, gerberas, lilies, carnations, roses etc.; bouquets; flower arrangements—fresh and dry etc. sometimes there are flowering plants for sale in decorative containers/pots)
- What have you noticed about the flowers in a florist? (They are usually cut flowers in an arrangement or gathered together to be arranged in a vase.)

Not all flower varieties are suitable to put in vases as they wilt quickly.

- Why do people buy cut flowers? (as gifts, to decorate homes/workplaces, for celebration venues, churches etc. Dried arrangements are used for the same purposes and may last for years.)

Lesson one ○●●●

Materials

- ★ • black card (23 cm x 34 cm)
- ★ • cartridge paper (15 cm x 21 cm)
- ★ • blue paper/card rectangle (16.5 cm x 10 cm)
- ★ • dark blue corrugated card (15 cm x 8 cm)
- ★ • gold corrugated card (7 cm x 4 cm)
- ★ • black card (4.5 cm x 3 cm)
- • coloured corrugated card scraps
- • paper punch
- • scissors
- • oil pastels—fluorescent
- • glue stick
- • hot glue gun
- • craft glue 250 mL (squeeze bottle)
- ★ • ribbon (3 mm width x 15 cm length)
- • glitter glue, gel pen etc.

Note: Where several glue types are listed, hot glue is the most effective, however, other glue types will suffice.

Method

1. Following discussion about florists, cut flowers and reasons for purchasing flowers, students use oil pastels to create squares of colour using a back and forth line colouring technique to make a check pattern on cartridge paper.
2. Fold large black card in half to make a greeting card.
3. Using glue stick, glue cartridge paper to the front of card.
4. Make a trapezium using the blue paper/card and dark blue corrugated card by measuring 2 cm from corners,

ruling a line and cutting along the line with scissors. Glue background pieces into position using glue stick generously.

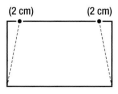
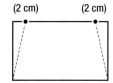

(2 cm) (2 cm) (2 cm) (2 cm)

Blue card/paper | Dark blue corrugated card
16.5 cm x 10 cm | 15 cm x 8 cm

5. Make a flower in a vase by drawing shapes on the back of coloured corrugated card and cutting out (see example).
6. Glue flower and vase into position using glue stick generously, craft glue or hot glue gun.
7. Rule lines on gold rectangle to taper the shape of the tag.

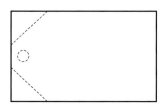

8. Cut along lines with scissors.
9. Punch a hole using paper punch.
10. Using glue stick, glue small rectangle of black card onto tag.
11. Thread ribbon through the hole and tie a bow.
12. Using hot glue gun or craft glue, glue tag into position.
13. Write greeting message onto the tag using glitter glue or gel pen. Set aside to dry.

Lesson two ●○●

Materials

- • cartridge paper or coloured card (15 cm x 21 cm)
- • glue stick
- • reflection and assessment photocopies
- • lead pencil
- • coloured pencils

Method

1. Using glue stick, glue insert into card (15 cm x 21 cm).
2. Using writing implement, write an appropriate message to the recipient.
3. Students complete reflection activity.
4. Teacher completes assessment record.

R.I.C. Publications/Prim-Ed Publishing

Corrugated card flower greeting card
Reflections

1. List four different items you might find in a florist shop.

    _____

    _____

2. List three reasons why a person might make a purchase at a florist shop.

    _____

    _____

    _____

3. Which part of this activity did you enjoy most? Give a reason for your answer.

    _____

    _____

    _____

    _____

4. Some flowers are not suitable to be displayed as cut flowers. Why?

    _____

5. List three occasions on which you could use your greeting card.

    _____

    _____

    _____

6. Corrugated card shapes may be used to build a picture of many objects. Using lead pencil, draw another design for a greeting card using shapes of corrugated card. Colour your design using pencils and write a title.

Corrugated card flower greeting card
Task assessment

Activity objectives
Arts ideas: *Creates artworks to express ideas.*
Arts skills and processes: *Uses a range of visual arts skills, techniques, procedures, practices and technologies.*
Arts responses: *Uses an aesthetic understanding to acknowledge, reflect on and assess the arts.*
Arts in society: *Demonstrates an understanding of the part that the arts play in society.*

Task
The students were instructed to make a corrugated card flower greeting card using a
range of skills, techniques, mediums and materials.

Assessment key			
✔ **yes** (has demonstrated achievement of this criterion)			
✗ **no** (has not demonstrated achievement of this criterion)			
● **inconsistent** (some evidence of achievement has been shown)			
Criterion			
The student is able to:	✔	✗	●
participate in discussion about florists, cut flowers and reasons for purchasing flowers.			
colour with strong, solid colour using oil pastels.			
fold card in half.			
measure, rule and cut background paper/card and corrugated card.			
glue background card into position with glue stick.			
draw shapes to make a flower in a vase.			
cut accurately using scissors.			
write appropriate cover message.			
write an appropriate message inside the greeting card.			
complete a reflection sheet based on his/her artwork.			
listen to and follow instructions.			
work cooperatively in an informal activity-based work environment.			

Primary art **9**

Metallic strip greeting card

This greeting card was inspired by the topic *Recycling*. The students had been exposed to the different forms of recycling and had been investigating ways to reduce wastage of precious natural resources. As a culmination of the recycling learning activities, this art piece was completed using mostly metallic paper offcuts from past lessons.

Accurate measurement is also a skill practised in this activity, thus maths is incorporated. This project is simple and effective. It may be used for any occasion; e.g. Father's Day, birthday, thank you, get well. The example shown was made for Father's Day.

Two-lesson project

Discussion points

- What is recycling? (reusing products, especially natural resources, by repeated use or reprocessing etc.)
- What can we do to recycle at home? (ensure that we correctly dispose of recyclable materials; e.g. recycling bins and outlets; wherever possible, return organic materials to the earth; e.g. turning vegetable matter into compost; avoid wasting paper etc.)
- What is a greeting card?
- Have you ever received a greeting card?
- Why were you given a greeting card?
- Have you ever given someone a greeting card? (List reasons why we have given or received greeting cards.)

Recycling paper products to make art projects can be a very effective way to recycle.

Lesson one

Materials

- ★ • *coloured card (32 cm x 21 cm)*
- ★ • *black card (15 cm x 20 cm)*
- *metallic card/paper offcuts and full sheets*
- *lead pencil*
- *ruler*
- *scissors*
- *glue stick*
- *glitter glue, gel pens etc.*
- *newspaper to protect workspace*

Method

1. Following discussion about recycling and greeting cards, students fold large piece of coloured card in half. Set aside.
2. Students measure, rule and cut various widths of card/paper strips. Emphasise accurate measuring and cutting for most effective design outcome.
3. Place metallic strips in position on pre-cut black card background, laying some over others. Leave a small area to write a decorative greeting message.
4. Using glue stick generously, glue strips into position.
5. Trim around edges neatly.
6. Using glue stick generously, attach black card to the front of folded coloured card.

7. Write appropriate message inside the greeting card.
8. Write greeting message using glitter glue or gel pen on the front of card. Set aside to dry.

Lesson two

Materials

- *reflection and assessment photocopies*
- *lead pencil*
- *coloured pencils*

Method

1. Students complete reflection activity.
2. Teacher completes assessment record.

Metallic strip greeting card

R.I.C. Publications/Prim-Ed Publishing

Metallic strip greeting card
Reflections

1. List six mediums, materials and tools you used to make your card. You may include different varieties of paper.

   _____

   _____

   _____

2. Which part of this activity did you enjoy most? Give a reason for your answer.

   _____

   _____

   _____

3. Were you able to measure, rule and cut out your metallic paper/card strips to your satisfaction?

Yes	No

   Give a reason for your answer.

   _____

   _____

   _____

4. List three reasons why it is important to recycle.

   _____

   _____

   _____

5. List five items you recycle at home.

   _____

   _____

6. Draw another greeting card featuring a shape instead of stripes and a range of paper types and colours. Label your design with the papers you have used. Colour your card with pencils.

R.I.C. Publications/Prim-Ed Publishing

Metallic strip greeting card
Task assessment

Activity objectives

Arts ideas: *Creates artworks to express ideas.*

Arts skills and processes: *Uses a range of visual arts skills, techniques, procedures, practices and technologies.*

Arts responses: *Uses an aesthetic understanding to acknowledge, reflect on and assess the arts.*

Arts in society: *Demonstrates an understanding of the part that the arts play in society.*

Task

The students were instructed to make a greeting card featuring metallic strips and using a range of skills, techniques, mediums and materials.

Assessment key		
✔ **yes** (has demonstrated achievement of this criterion)		
✗ **no** (has not demonstrated achievement of this criterion)		
● **inconsistent** (some evidence of achievement has been shown)		
Criterion		
The student is able to:	✔	✗	●
participate in class discussion about recycling and greeting cards.			
fold card in half accurately.			
measure and rule strips of paper/card accurately.			
cut along measured and ruled lines accurately using scissors.			
glue metallic paper/card strips into position on black card background.			
trim around edges of the background.			
glue decorated background onto the front of greeting card.			
write greeting message inside card.			
write greeting message on front of card.			
complete a reflection sheet based on his/her artwork.			
listen to and follow instructions.			
work cooperatively in an informal activity-based work environment.			

Primary art 13

Etched name leaning board

This lesson was inspired by the need for a durable leaning mat and as a follow-up to a 'getting to know you' oral activity at the beginning of the year. Using people's names respectfully (an area of social values) was also integrated.

Note: A leaning board is a protective mat similar to a placemat.

Three-lesson project

Discussion points

- What name do you prefer to be called? (some students will prefer nicknames)
- What is a nickname? (any name other than the name a person is given at birth/on their birth certificate) Nicknames may be a different name, a short form of the real name, either first or last name, an endearment etc.
- When is it okay to use a nickname? (when the person has encouraged you to use it; when you are using it in a positive manner etc.)

Lesson one

Materials

- ★ A3 cartridge paper (trim 2 cm from the length and 2 cm from the width)
- ★ overhead transparency of letter shapes page 131, (optional)
- lead pencil
- oil pastels
- black acrylic paint
- polystyrene trays (for paint)
- paintbrushes (medium and fine)
- newspaper to protect workspace

Method

1. Following discussion about names and nicknames, distribute cartridge paper.

2. Using lead pencil, students write names decoratively. (Use overhead transparency of page 131 if desired.)

3. Using oil pastels, colour letters with strong, solid colour (no black).

4. Paint over entire surface using black paint and a soft-bristle brush. Emphasise even coverage—no puddles. Set aside to dry.

Lesson two

Materials

- artwork in progress
- matchsticks
- card for mounting
- A3 laminating sheets
- newspaper to protect workspace

Method

1. Using a matchstick, scratch/etch patterns onto letters. Create a different pattern for each letter. A faint outline can be seen.

★ 2. Enlist adult help to mount completed artwork onto coloured card and laminate to enhance durability.

Lesson three

Materials

- reflection and assessment photocopies
- lead pencil
- coloured pencils

Method

1. Students complete reflection activity.

2. Teacher completes assessment record.

R.I.C. Publications/Prim-Ed Publishing

Etched name leaning board

Etched name leaning board
Reflections

1. List five materials, mediums and tools you used to make your etched name leaning board.

_____

_____

_____

2. Which part of this activity did you enjoy most? Give a reason for your answer.

_____

_____

_____

3. Write the instructions someone would need to complete this activity.

_____

_____

_____

_____

4. Using lead pencil, draw a scene which you would like to etch into a prepared surface. Colour the picture revealed by your etching.

R.I.C. Publications/Prim-Ed Publishing

Etched name leaning board
Task assessment

Activity objectives

Arts ideas: *Creates artworks to express ideas.*

Arts skills and processes: *Uses a range of visual arts skills, techniques, procedures, practices and technologies.*

Arts responses: *Uses an aesthetic understanding to acknowledge, reflect on and assess the arts.*

Arts in society: *Demonstrates an understanding of the part that the arts play in society.*

Task

The students were instructed to make an etched name leaning board using a range of skills, techniques, mediums and materials

Assessment key			
✔ **yes** (has demonstrated achievement of this criterion)			
✗ **no** (has not demonstrated achievement of this criterion)			
● **inconsistent** (some evidence of achievement has been shown)			
Criterion			
The student is able to:	✔	✗	●
participate in class discussion about names and nicknames.			
draw his/her name using decorative lettering.			
colour lettering with strong, solid colour using oil pastels.			
paint over entire page using acrylic paint and paintbrush.			
etch patterns onto letters.			
complete a reflection sheet based on his/her artwork.			
listen to and follow instructions.			
work cooperatively in an informal activity-based work environment.			

Primary art | **17**

Metallic space scene

This activity was inspired by the theme *Space,* with a focus on 'textures' and the harsh environments of other planets.

Three-lesson project

Discussion points

Pictures or photos of planets will inspire meaningful discussion. The planets discovered so far cannot support human life (without major infrastructure) because of the harsh environments.

- What do you know about the environments of most planets? (They have varied harsh environments which could not, unassisted, support human life etc.)

The artwork will be a picture of an imaginary planet. This planet's landscape will have interesting textures, created using a range of tools and metallic paint.

- How might we make textures using paint? (Brainstorm ideas and suggestions on how to make textures, drawing on students' knowledge and experiences gained during previous lessons.) It is important to demonstrate a range of techniques following discussion. See 'Painting techniques'.
- How can we create depth/distance in a picture? (making objects/detail smaller in the background; overlapping picture parts)

Lesson one

Materials

- A3 cartridge paper (2 sheets)
- acrylic paint (variety of metallic and standard colours)
- scrap cardboard (small pieces approx. 8 cm x 8 cm)
- scissors
- paintbrushes (thick, medium, fine and flat-bristled)
- polystyrene trays (for paint)
- newspaper to protect workspace

Method

1. Following discussion about colours, teacher demonstrates a range of painting techniques which create 'texture' (see below).
2. Students loosely fold A3 cartridge paper into quarters widthwise.

3. Students paint one-quarter at a time, using different colours and a range of textures from the techniques outlined in discussion or teacher demonstration. Encourage experimentation. Set aside to dry. (Eight different sets to be created.)

Lesson two

Materials

- artwork in progress
- A4 photocopy paper
- lead pencil
- A3 cartridge paper
- scissors
- glue stick
- black card for mounting
- craft glue for mounting
- newspaper to protect workspace

Method

1. Using lead pencil, design a plan of a space scene on A4 paper, using available painted textures.
2. Cut textured paper to shape, bearing in mind the size of the background.
3. Continue this process, positioning and building picture.
4. Using glue stick, glue pieces into position. Set aside to dry.
★ 5. Enlist adult help to trim and mount work onto black card.

Lesson three

Materials

- artwork in progress
- craft glue for mounting
- paintbrush (fine)
- glitter (gold or copper)
- newspaper to protect workspace
- reflection and assessment photocopies
- lead pencil
- coloured pencils

Method

1. Using fine paintbrush, craft glue and glitter, add flame detail.
2. Students complete reflection activity.
3. Teacher completes assessment record.

Painting techniques

Use a flat-bristled paintbrush to paint short strokes in various directions.	Paint an area of thick colour, then scratch/etch into it with the handle of a fine paintbrush.	Cut notches into a piece of scrap card. Scrape card across a painted area to make lines or curves.

Metallic space scene

Metallic space scene
Reflections

1. Which part of this activity did you enjoy most? Give a reason for your answer.

   _____

   _____

   _____

2. Draw the textures you used to create your metallic space scene picture. Label each texture with the tool you used to create the effect.

3. What technique did you use in your design to create depth/distance in your picture?

   _____

   _____

   _____

4. Using lead pencil, draw another scene, using textures to enhance your picture. Colour your drawing. Label the textures with the tool you would use to create the effect.

R.I.C. Publications/Prim-Ed Publishing

Metallic space scene
Task assessment

Activity objectives

Arts ideas: *Creates artworks to express ideas.*

Arts skills and processes: *Uses a range of visual arts skills, techniques, procedures, practices and technologies.*

Arts responses: *Uses an aesthetic understanding to acknowledge, reflect on and assess the arts.*

Arts in society: *Demonstrates an understanding of the part that the arts play in society.*

Task

The students were instructed to make a textured painting space scene using a range of skills, techniques, mediums and materials.

Assessment key			
✔ **yes** *(has demonstrated achievement of this criterion)*			
✗ **no** *(has not demonstrated achievement of this criterion)*			
● **inconsistent** *(some evidence of achievement has been shown)*			
Criterion			
The student is able to:	✔	✗	●
participate in discussion about space, harsh environments, texture effects in painting and how to create depth in a picture.			
paint textures using eight techniques.			
draw a plan of a textured painting space scene.			
build a space scene picture by cutting and pasting textured painting pieces.			
create depth in picture by overlapping picture pieces and/or making objects/ detail smaller in the background.			
enhance space scene picture with glitter highlights.			
complete a reflection sheet based on his/her artwork.			
listen to and follow instructions.			
work cooperatively in an informal activity-based work environment.			

Primary art 21

Repetitive drawing sea animal collage

This lesson can be related to any theme; the guidelines change according to the topic. The theme for the example shown was *The sea*.

Three-lesson project

Discussion points

Stimulus pictures and clip art of sea animals are a useful resource to assist students with their initial drawing.

- What animals live in the sea? (shellfish, whales, fish etc.)
- What is your favourite sea animal? (Answers will vary.)
- What characteristics does your sea animal have? (e.g. shell, fins, tail)
- What colour/colours is your favourite sea animal? (Answers will vary.)

Lesson one

Materials

- A3 cartridge paper
- A5 photocopy paper
- ★ clip art of sea animals made into an overhead transparency if desired
- lead pencil
- thick permanent black marker
- newspaper to protect workspace

Method

1. Following discussion about sea animals, students select one animal as a master for the collage.
2. Using lead pencil, students draw the selected sea animal onto A5 paper.
3. When satisfied with the result, students trace over pencil outline using permanent black marker. This is the 'master' drawing.
4. Students trace master sea animal design onto A3 cartridge paper, either directly with black marker or with lead pencil first, followed by permanent black marker. Repeat tracing, adding depth by overlapping each. Cover page with animals. Emphasise that the overlapped area of the picture is not to be traced.

Lesson two

Materials

- artwork in progress
- colouring mediums – acrylic paint
  - Edicol™ vegetable dye
  - paintbrush (fine)
  - watercolour pencils—water
  - water container
  - wax crayons
- newspaper to protect workspace
- card for mounting
- craft glue for mounting

Method

1. Complete tracings if necessary.
2. Colour single tracing which isn't overlapped by any other tracing. (This will be the original tracing.) Use any of the colouring mediums available.
3. Colour background using any of the available mediums. (Example shown was coloured with watercolour pencil.) If required, set aside to dry.
★ 4. Enlist adult help to mount work onto coloured card (optional).

Lesson three

Materials

- reflection and assessment photocopies
- lead pencil
- coloured pencils

Method

1. Students complete reflection activity.
2. Teacher completes assessment record.

R.I.C. Publications/Prim-Ed Publishing

R.I.C. Publications/Prim-Ed Publishing

Repetitive drawing sea animal collage
Reflections

1. Which sea animal did you draw? _____

2. What did you enjoy most about this activity? Give a reason for your answer.

    _____

    _____

    _____

3. Which part of this activity was most challenging?

    _____

    Why? _____

    _____

    _____

    _____

4. Which colouring medium did you use to colour the initial tracing?

    _____

5. Were you satisfied with the finished effect? | Yes | No |

    Give a reason for your answer.

    _____

    _____

6. Draw an object of your choice which would make an effective master drawing for another repetitive collage. Label the drawing to show the colouring mediums you would use.

Repetitive drawing sea animal collage
Task assessment

Activity objectives

Arts ideas: *Creates artworks to express ideas.*

Arts skills and processes: *Uses a range of visual arts skills, techniques, procedures, practices and technologies.*

Arts responses: *Uses an aesthetic understanding to acknowledge, reflect on and assess the arts.*

Arts in society: *Demonstrates an understanding of the part that the arts play in society.*

Task

The students were instructed to make a sea animal drawing collage using a range of skills, techniques, mediums and materials.

Assessment key			
✔ **yes** (has demonstrated achievement of this criterion)			
✗ **no** (has not demonstrated achievement of this criterion)			
● **inconsistent** (some evidence of achievement has been shown)			
Criterion			
The student is able to:	✔	✗	●
participate in discussion about sea animals.			
draw a picture of a sea animal.			
trace his/her drawing many times onto A3 cartridge paper to form a repetitive drawing collage.			
demonstrate depth in picture by overlapping tracings accurately.			
use a colouring medium to complete initial tracing.			
colour background using a chosen medium.			
complete a reflection sheet based on his/her artwork.			
listen to and follow instructions.			
work cooperatively in an informal activity-based work environment.			

Primary art **25**

Summer fabric design

This project was inspired by an interest in fashion design demonstrated by a group of students. An emphasis was placed on bright and breezy colours which reflect the light nature of summer clothing. The design theme for the example shown was flowers; however, any design is appropriate; e.g. car shapes, rocket shapes, umbrella shapes etc.

Four-lesson project

Discussion points

As a stimulus for discussion and comparison, bring in several articles of summer and winter clothing.

- What is the difference between summer and winter clothing?
- What are the characteristics of each?
  - ~ *Summer: lightweight, tend to have a focus on bright colours, designed for coolness.*
  - ~ *Winter: heavyweight, tend to have a focus on dark colours, designed for warming qualities.*
- What methods/techniques could be used to create fabric designs? (screen printing, sketching, drawing, painting, tissue shapes etc.)

The example shown was created using a tissue shape with a flower theme.

Lesson one

Materials
- recycled cardboard
- lead pencil
- scissors
- tissue paper (variety of colours)
- envelopes to store tissue shapes

Method
1. Following discussion about summer and winter clothing characteristics and colour, choose a theme shape.
2. Using lead pencil, students draw variations of the shape onto cardboard to make templates for tracing. (These should vary in shape and size.)
3. Using scissors, cut out shape templates.
4. Using lead pencil, trace template shapes onto tissue paper.
5. Cut out tissue paper shapes. (Store shapes in a named envelope ready for Lesson two.)

Lesson two

Materials
- artwork in progress
- A3 cartridge paper
- diluted craft glue (1 part water to 3 parts craft glue)
- polystyrene trays (for craft glue)
- glue brush
- newspaper to protect workspace
- card for mounting
- craft glue for mounting (undiluted)

Method
1. Complete tracing and cutting tissue shapes.
2. Brush entire A3 cartridge paper with glue.
3. Place tissue paper shapes on the page and paint over them with glue solution to smooth down the edges.
4. Place more shapes onto paper, overlapping if desired.
5. Smooth down edges by brushing with glue solution. Set aside to dry.
★ 6. Enlist adult help to trim the edges using a slide cutter if available and to mount work onto coloured card (optional).

Lesson three

Materials
- artwork in progress
- thin permanent black marker
- thick permanent black marker
- craft glue for mounting
- paintbrush (fine)
- polystyrene trays (for glue)
- glitter (optional)
- newspaper to protect workspace

Method
1. Add detail to tissue shapes using fine black and thick permanent black markers.
2. Enhance detail by painting craft glue using a fine brush and sprinkling with glitter (if desired). Emphasise that 'more is not always best'. Set aside to dry.

Lesson four

Materials
- reflection and assessment photocopies
- lead pencil
- coloured pencils

Method
1. Students complete reflection activity.
2. Teacher completes assessment record.

Summer fabric design

R.I.C. Publications/Prim-Ed Publishing

Summer fabric design
Reflections

1. List six mediums, materials and tools you used to make your summer fabric design.

   _____

   _____

   _____

2. Which part of the activity did you enjoy most? Give a reason for your answer.

   _____

   _____

   _____

3. Explain why you chose the design you created.

   _____

   _____

4. List two articles of clothing on which the design you have created would look effective.

   _____

   _____

5. Using lead pencil, draw two garments which could be made using the design you have created. Colour your designs with pencils.

Summer fabric design
Task assessment

Activity objectives

Arts ideas: *Creates artworks to express ideas.*

Arts skills and processes: *Uses a range of visual arts skills, techniques, procedures, practices and technologies.*

Arts responses: *Uses an aesthetic understanding to acknowledge, reflect on and assess the arts.*

Arts in society: *Demonstrates an understanding of the part that the arts play in society.*

Task

The students were instructed to make a summer fabric design using a range of
skills, techniques, mediums and materials.

Assessment key			
✔ **yes** (has demonstrated achievement of this criterion)			
✗ **no** (has not demonstrated achievement of this criterion)			
● **inconsistent** (some evidence of achievement has been shown)			
Criterion			
The student is able to:	✔	✗	●
participate in discussion about the characteristics of summer and winter clothing and techniques used to design and colour fabrics.			
draw shapes related to a chosen theme to make templates for tracing.			
trace template shapes onto tissue paper.			
cut shapes with scissors.			
glue edges of tissue shapes smoothly.			
add detail to design using markers.			
complete a reflection sheet based on his/her artwork.			
listen to and follow instructions.			
work cooperatively in an informal activity-based work environment.			

R.I.C. Publications/Prim-Ed Publishing

Slipping and sliding

This project is a quick and effective activity which adds instant colour to the classroom. Photos from magazines, calendars and pamphlets form the base for the picture. The students view and compare sports articles in a variety of publications, newspapers, magazines, advertising leaflets and timetables for sporting events. They then choose a photo of a person or object related to a sport theme.

Effective advertising was a focus in a viewing lesson leading up to this art activity. Appropriate material may be collected by making a request; for example, in the school newsletter weeks in advance.

Two lesson project

Discussion points

Photos of various sports from a range of publications will inspire meaningful discussion.

- Which sports did you read about while viewing the sports publications provided?
  (List sporting activities on the board.)
- Which sport is your favourite sport? Is it one you participate in or simply enjoy watching?
- Action shots are very eye-catching. What style of photo caught your attention?
- Eye-catching photos are used for several reasons. What might these reasons be? (to promote interest in a sport; to enhance the advertising effect for the sponsor of the sport; to promote interest in the person participating in the sport etc.)
- Many effects can be created by changing the appearance of a photo using computer technology. This activity changes a photo by giving it a striped effect. Demonstrate measuring, ruling and cutting 1-cm stripes on the back of a picture.

Lesson one

Materials

- sport publications—magazines, sporting events timetables, newspapers, leaflets advertising an event etc.
- coloured card (A4/A3) depending on size of photo chosen for activity
- lead pencil
- ruler
- scissors
- glue stick
- newspaper to protect workspace
- card for mounting
- craft glue for mounting

Method

1. Following discussion about sports and effective photos, students choose and cut out a photo/picture which is 'eye-catching'.
2. Students measure and rule 1-cm stripes on the back of the photo/picture.
3. Using scissors, cut carefully along the lines. Emphasise that accuracy is essential to attain the best effect.
4. Arrange strips of photo/picture in correct order on coloured card.
5. Using glue stick, attach strips in place, positioning alternate strips 1 cm lower. This will create an effect of stripes and an illusion that the stripes have slipped out of place.
★ 6. Enlist adult assistance to mount work onto coloured card.

Lesson two

Materials

- reflection and assessment photocopies
- lead pencil
- coloured pencils

Method

1. Students complete reflection activity.
2. Teacher completes assessment record.

R.I.C. Publications/Prim-Ed Publishing

Slipping and sliding
Reflections

1. List six materials and tools you used to make your slipping and sliding photo/picture.

   _____

   _____

2. Which part of this activity did you enjoy most? Give a reason for your answer.

   _____

   _____

   _____

3. When you were looking through sport publications, which style of photo did you find most eye-catching? Give a reason for your answer.

   _____

   _____

   _____

4. Make a set of instructions which another person could follow to complete this art project.

   _____

   _____

   _____

   _____

   _____

   _____

5. Using lead pencil, draw/design a full-page advertisement for an item of sports equipment. Colour your advertisement. Remember to use effective, eye-catching colour.

R.I.C. Publications/Prim-Ed Publishing

Name: .... Year: .... Date: ....

Slipping and sliding
Task assessment

Activity objectives

Arts ideas: *Creates artworks to express ideas.*

Arts skills and processes: *Uses a range of visual arts skills, techniques, procedures, practices and technologies.*

Arts responses: *Uses an aesthetic understanding to acknowledge, reflect on and assess the arts.*

Arts in society: *Demonstrates an understanding of the part that the arts play in society.*

Task

The students were instructed to make a picture featuring a sport-related photo/picture, using a range of skills, techniques and materials.

Assessment key			
✔ **yes** *(has demonstrated achievement of this criterion)*			
✗ **no** *(has not demonstrated achievement of this criterion)*			
● **inconsistent** *(some evidence of achievement has been shown)*			
Criterion			
The student is able to:	✔	✗	●
participate in discussion about sport publications articles, photos and effective use of photos in advertising.			
measure and rule straight 1-cm wide strips on the back of a selected photo/ picture.			
cut along straight lines accurately with scissors.			
glue strips into position, positioning alternate strips 1 cm lower.			
complete a reflection sheet based on his/her artwork.			
listen to and follow instructions.			
work cooperatively in an informal activity-based work environment.			

Primary art **33**

Porthole scene

The theme *Pirates* initiated this lesson. After the reading of a pirate story, discussion followed about the sea, what it may be like travelling by ship and what could be seen from a porthole.

Three-lesson project

Discussion points

- What is a lighthouse? (a tall building with a strong lamp at the top)
- Where are lighthouses found? (Often, lighthouses are located on dangerous, rocky coastal areas where ships/boats could be in danger.)
- What might you see from the porthole of a ship? (the sea, seabirds, other ships, an island, a lighthouse etc.)
- What colours can you see when you look at the sea? (blues, greens)
- Why does the ocean change colour? (cloud cover creates more green tones; clear blue sky gives more blue tones)

Lesson one

Materials

- ★ cartridge paper photocopy of circle shape
- ★ photocopy paper disc as above (for plan)
- cartridge paper scraps
- ★ grey card (approximately 15 cm x 5 cm)
- ★ prepared lighthouse template (optional) (page 132)
- egg cartons (to build a rocky shore)
- soup mix
- scissors
- metallic paper scraps
- Edicol™ dye (sea and sky colours: blues and greens)
- acrylic paint (variety of colours)
- paintbrushes (medium and fine)
- craft glue 250 mL (squeeze bottle)
- lead pencil
- newspaper to protect workspace

Method

1. Following discussion, students use lead pencil to draw on scrap paper a plan of a scene which may be seen from a porthole.
2. Paint cartridge paper disc with darker shades of blue dye on the bottom half and a lighter blue sky on the top half. Set aside to dry.
3. Paint paper scraps with shades of blue dye (3-D waves). Set aside to dry.
4. Tear egg carton into small pieces to make a rocky foundation and use craft glue generously to attach in position.
5. Glue soup mix around rocks. Set aside to dry.
6. Using lead pencil, draw a lighthouse onto grey card (or use template p. 132).

7. Paint detail onto lighthouse using paint (door, light, roof, railings) and make metallic paper windows.
8. Glue windows to lighthouse using glue stick.

Lesson two

Materials

- artwork in progress
- ★ prepared corrugated card disc (approx. 28 cm in diameter)
- brown acrylic paint
- paintbrushes (medium and fine)
- coins (2 sizes) (to represent nuts and bolts holding porthole in position)
- black and blue paper/card scraps
- cardboard or foam packaging
- silver metallic paper
- wadding/stuffing
- glue stick
- craft glue for mounting
- glitter (gold)
- fine permanent black marker
- scissors
- newspaper to protect workspace

Method

1. Using fine permanent black marker, draw detail onto lighthouse picture.
2. Cut out sea picture and glue to corrugated card.
3. Cut out and attach blue paper scrap waves, gluing only at the bottom.
4. Use craft glue to attach packaging underneath lighthouse in position.
5. Paint rocky foundation carefully with brown paint.
6. Add rays of light with craft glue and glitter. (Avoid wet brown shore.)
7. Glue on wadding for mist.
8. Use lead pencil to trace eight large coins on back of black paper/card and eight small coins on silver metallic paper.
9. Cut out and, using glue stick, glue silver discs on top of black ones, then glue evenly around porthole.

Lesson three

Materials

- reflection and assessment photocopies
- coloured pencils
- lead pencil

Method

1. Students complete reflection activity.
2. Teacher completes assessment record.

R.I.C. Publications/Prim-Ed Publishing

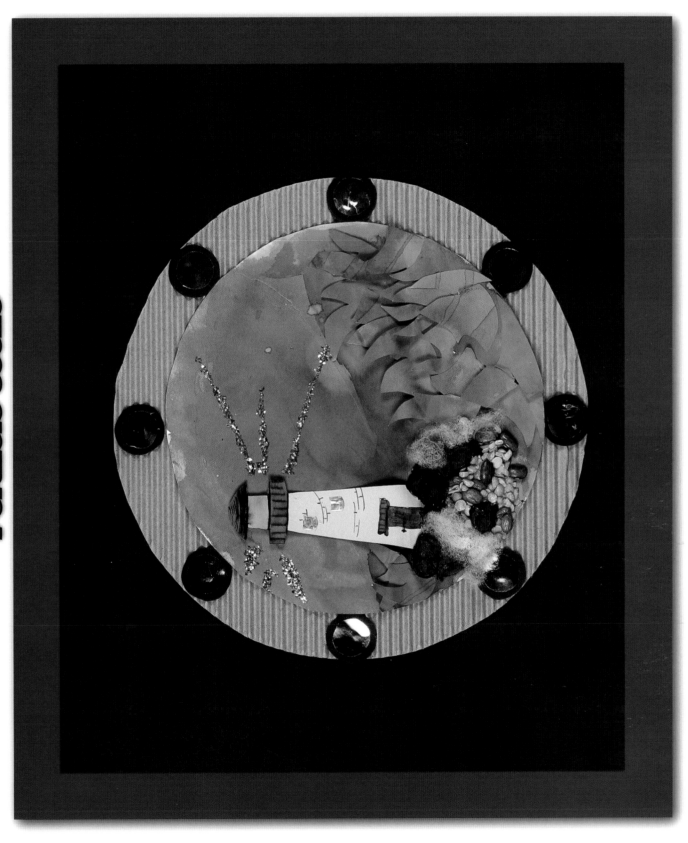

R.I.C. Publications/Prim-Ed Publishing

Porthole scene
Reflections

1. Which part of the activity did you enjoy most? Give a reason for your answer.

   _____

   _____

2. Draw the scene you might see from your porthole and label your drawing, showing the materials and techniques you used to represent each feature on your art piece.

   [drawing box]

3. List two factors which affect the colour of the sea.

   _____   _____

4. Why is it important for a lighthouse lamp to be functioning correctly?

   _____

   _____

5. Apart from the scene you created, what else might you see from a porthole while you were out to sea?

   _____

   _____

6. Using lead pencil, draw a scene showing what may happen if a lighthouse light fails to work on a stormy night. Colour your drawing with pencils.

   [drawing box]

R.I.C. Publications/Prim-Ed Publishing

Porthole scene
Task assessment

Activity objectives

Arts ideas: *Creates artworks to express ideas.*

Arts skills and processes: *Uses a range of visual arts skills, techniques, procedures, practices and technologies.*

Arts responses: *Uses an aesthetic understanding to acknowledge, reflect on and assess the arts.*

Arts in society: *Demonstrates an understanding of the part that the arts play in society.*

Task

The students were instructed to make a porthole sea scene using a range of skills, techniques, mediums and materials.

Assessment key			
✔ **yes** (has demonstrated achievement of this criterion)			
✘ **no** (has not demonstrated achievement of this criterion)			
● **inconsistent** (some evidence of achievement has been shown)			
Criterion			
The student is able to:	✔	✘	●
participate in class discussion about pirates, lighthouses, the sea and what can be seen from a ship.			
make a plan/design of a scene which may be seen from a porthole.			
use a minimum of three techniques to make a sea scene picture.			
make a sea scene picture effectively.			
complete a reflection sheet based on his/her artwork.			
listen to and follow instructions.			
work cooperatively in an informal activity-based work environment.			

Across the street

Three-lesson project

Discussion points

Stimulus pictures of terrace housing, if available, would promote creativity.

- What is terrace housing? (a series of two-storey or taller houses with at least one common wall)
- What makes a terrace house different from a single-storey home? (Points to consider: more compact living, traditional room layout, entries and windows at front and back, common walls, effective use of small blocks of land etc.)
- Who could comfortably live in a townhouse? (couples, small families, single people; not very suitable for large families and people who like to have a large pet)

Inner-city living in terrace housing has become more popular in recent years. This is partly because the very design of common-wall, multistorey dwellings saves space.

Although traditional terrace houses have many common features, they can look very different because of individual decorative features, which add character to the appearance. These include wide and varied roof lines, windows—size and shape—balconies, ballustrades, lofts, door style, colour, texture—brick, rendered etc.

Drawing a scene with depth requires drawing the foreground first and building the picture from there. This may be demonstrated on the board. If you lived in a terrace house, what might you see from your front window—your view across the street? (other terrace houses, some grassland, a small stream, bridge etc.)

Emphasis: The drawing must include some terrace housing.

Lesson one

Materials

- A4 photocopy paper
- A3 cartridge paper
- lead pencil
- eraser
- ruler
- newspaper to protect workspace
- permanent black marker

Method

1. Following discussion about terrace houses and what we might see across the street from our front window, and using lead pencil and A4 paper, students draw a series of terrace houses and surrounding scenery, including any other features. Students should use ideas discussed as inspiration.

   Emphasise that this is a plan only and should be a quick, rough outline for the main art piece.

2. Using lead pencil, draw scene onto A3 cartridge paper.

3. When satisfied with drawing, go over lines with permanent black marker.

Lesson two

Materials

- artwork in progress
- equipment from Lesson one if some students have not completed drawing their 'across the road' scene
- wax crayons
- oil pastels
- water soluble oil pastels (optional)
- card for mounting
- craft glue for mounting
- newspaper to protect workspace

Method

1. Commence colouring 'across the road' scene using wax crayons and/or oil pastels.

★ 2. Enlist adult help to mount completed work (optional).

Lesson three

Materials

- reflection and assessment photocopies
- lead pencil
- coloured pencils

Method

1. Students complete reflection activity.

2. Teacher completes assessment record.

R.I.C. Publications/Prim-Ed Publishing

Across the street
Reflections

1. Why are terrace houses suitable for inner city living?

   _____

   _____

2. Did you follow the plan you drew for your picture? | Yes | No |

   Give a reason for your answer. _____

   _____

3. Apart from terrace houses, what features did you include in your 'across the street' picture?

   _____

   _____

4. Which part of this activity did you enjoy most? Give a reason for your answer.

   _____

   _____

5. Would you like to live in the street you have designed? Why/Why not?

   _____

   _____

   _____

6. Draw a plan for a modern day terrace house scene.

R.I.C. Publications/Prim-Ed Publishing

Across the street
Task assessment

Activity objectives

Arts ideas: *Creates artworks to express ideas.*

Arts skills and processes: *Uses a range of visual arts skills, techniques, procedures, practices and technologies.*

Arts responses: *Uses an aesthetic understanding to acknowledge, reflect on and assess the arts.*

Arts in society: *Demonstrates an understanding of the part that the arts play in society.*

Task

The students were instructed to draw and colour a terrace housing street scene which could be seen from a window across the road.

Assessment key			
✔ **yes** (has demonstrated achievement of this criterion)			
✘ **no** (has not demonstrated achievement of this criterion)			
● **inconsistent** (some evidence of achievement has been shown)			
Criterion			
The student is able to:	✔	✘	●
participate in discussion about terrace houses and suburban street features.			
draw a plan of a terrace housing street scene.			
transfer plan drawing to larger picture.			
trace over drawing with permanent black marker.			
demonstrate strong, solid colouring using wax crayons and/or oil pastels.			
complete a reflection sheet based on his/her artwork.			
listen to and follow instructions.			
work cooperatively in an informal activity-based work environment.			

Chalk pastels star collage

This project was inspired by the theme *Space.* The topic of *Stars* was studied when covering the solar system, meteorites and comets.

Two-lesson project

Discussion points ○○○

- What are stars? (any of the self-luminous bodies outside of the solar system; although stars are not figures with five points, they are luminous and tend to appear as a 'sparkle'; when we draw them, we represent them with points to give them the illusion of a sparkle)

Stars are associated with decorations, to draw attention. They are used to enhance and make things/ objects stand out; e.g. Christmas decorations, lights, stickers for good work etc.

Stars are connected with analogies which relate to bright lights; e.g. after a bang on the head, someone may see stars etc.

Lesson two ○

Materials
- *reflection and assessment photocopies*
- *lead pencil*
- *coloured pencils*

Method
1. Students complete reflection activity.
2. Teacher completes assessment record.

Lesson one ○○

Materials
- *A3 cartridge paper*
- *chalk pastels*
- *hair spray (to reduce smudging)*
- *craft glue for mounting*
- *coloured card for mounting*
- *newspaper to protect workspace*

Method
1. Following discussion about stars, and using chalk pastels, teacher demonstrates how to draw a five-point star.

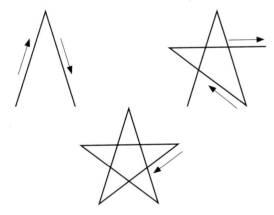

2. Students draw three stars, spaced around the sheet of A3 cartridge paper, using chalk pastels.
3. Add colour by drawing lines inside each star as shown in example.
4. Fill surrounding space by drawing concentric lines with different colours.
★ 5. Enlist adult help to spray completed pictures with hair spray. This will reduce smudging.
★ 6. Enlist adult help to mount work onto coloured card.

R.I.C. Publications/Prim-Ed Publishing

Chalk pastels star collage

Chalk pastels star collage
Reflections

1. List three things you know about stars.

_____

_____

_____

2. Which part of this activity did you enjoy most? Give a reason for your answer.

_____

_____

_____

3. Why are stars associated with decorations?

_____

_____

4. Chalk pastels are a very soft drawing medium, which smudges easily. What can we do to prevent a chalk pastel drawing from smudging?

_____

_____

5. Many different gift items could be decorated with a star collage design. Draw two gift items which could be decorated with stars. Colour your drawings.

<table>
<tr><td>

</td><td></td></tr>
</table>

R.I.C. Publications/Prim-Ed Publishing

Chalk pastels star collage
Task assessment

Activity objectives

Arts ideas: *Creates artworks to express ideas.*

Arts skills and processes: *Uses a range of visual arts skills, techniques, procedures, practices and technologies.*

Arts responses: *Uses an aesthetic understanding to acknowledge, reflect on and assess the arts.*

Arts in society: *Demonstrates an understanding of the part that the arts play in society.*

Task

The students were instructed to draw a star collage using chalk pastels.

Assessment key			
✔ **yes** (has demonstrated achievement of this criterion)			
✗ **no** (has not demonstrated achievement of this criterion)			
● **inconsistent** (some evidence of achievement has been shown)			
Criterion			
The student is able to:	✔	✗	●
participate in discussion about stars and associated characteristics.			
draw stars with chalk pastels.			
draw concentric lines with chalk pastels.			
complete a reflection sheet based on his/her artwork.			
listen to and follow instructions.			
work cooperatively in an informal activity-based work environment.			

Butterfly farm

This activity was inspired by the theme *Insects* with a focus on 'butterflies'. A combination of 2-D and 3-D creates a realistic illusion of butterflies on a leafy background. Butterflies are attracted to colourful plants and flowers and this characteristic leads into the themes of colour and seasons. The maths concept of *symmetry* is also incorporated in this project.

Three-lesson project

Discussion points ● ● ○

A poster of the colour wheel showing primary, secondary and tertiary colours will inspire meaningful discussion.

- In which season of the year do most flowers bloom? (spring)
- What mini beasts live in the garden? (List these on the board.)
- What is an insect? Discuss characteristics: arthropod with three distinct body parts—head, thorax and abdomen; three pairs of legs; and usually wings. Which mini beasts are insects? (ants, beetles, bees, butterflies etc.)
- Butterflies flutter around the garden. What have you noticed about their wings? (They are the same on both sides—symmetrical. They are brightly coloured etc.)
- Why do you think butterflies are brightly coloured? (to camouflage themselves among the plants/flowers etc.)
- What are butterflies helping to do as they flutter from one flower to the next? (They transfer pollen, helping plants to pollinate and produce seeds for new plants.)
- What colours are butterflies? (all colours of the spectrum)
- Why do you think most people like butterflies? (They are colourful and beautiful to look at. They also help to keep our plants multiplying.)
- How could we encourage butterflies to come to our garden? (Plant lots of plants with colourful flowers; water regularly to create a damp environment etc.)
- What is a butterfly farm? (an enclosure where an environment/habitat has been created for the comfort and breeding of butterflies; usually open to the public in a similar fashion to the zoo)
- Which colours are warm colours? (red, orange, yellow, tan etc.)

Lesson one ● ●

Materials

- A4 cartridge paper (3 sheets per student)
- oil pastels (fluorescent colours if available)
- Edicol™ dye (sky blue)
- ★ prepared butterfly template (optional) (page 133)
- ★ recycled cardboard (approximately 9 cm x 9 cm)
- paintbrush (medium)
- scissors
- lead pencil
- newspaper to protect workspace
- card for mounting
- craft glue for mounting

Method

1. Following discussion, students use light green oil pastel to draw three leaves spaced around one sheet of A4 cartridge paper. (Emphasise strong, solid lines.) To create a realistic colour, draw and colour leaf centres with dark green oil pastel and smudge gently from centre outwards.
2. Paint remaining background with blue dye. Set aside to dry.
3. Repeat drawing and colouring of three leaves on second A4 sheet of cartridge paper.
4. Students draw their own butterfly shapes on recycled cardboard or use a photocopy of the butterfly shape (p. 133) to make a template.
5. Cut out butterfly shape.
6. Using lead pencil, students trace butterfly onto remaining sheet of A4 cartridge paper five times. (Odd numbers are always more aesthetically pleasing.)
7. Using warm colours (yellow, orange and red) and strong, solid colouring, colour butterfly wings using oil pastels with a back and forth line colouring technique to form stripes of colour. Vary the order of colours on each butterfly (as shown in example). Gently blend colours by smudging from the centre outwards.

★ 8. Enlist adult help to mount background onto coloured card before Lesson two.

Lesson two ● ●

Materials

- artwork in progress
- oil pastels (fluorescent if available)
- scissors
- hot glue guns or glue stick
- fine permanent black marker
- newspaper to protect workspace

Method

1. Complete colouring butterflies if unfinished.
2. Cut out butterflies and leaves on undyed page.
3. Using hot glue gun or glue stick generously, glue leaves into position on background, gently bending them to create a 3-D effect. (Glue gun provides a more durable result.) Set aside to dry.
4. Draw body detail using fine permanent black marker. (Remaining detail may be completed when butterfly has been glued onto background.)
5. Fold butterflies in half, position and glue them onto background using hot glue or glue stick generously.
6. Draw continuation of body and antennae using fine permanent black marker. Set aside to dry.

Lesson three ○

Materials

- reflection and assessment photocopies
- lead pencil
- coloured pencils

Method

1. Students complete reflection activity.
2. Teacher completes assessment record.

Butterfly farm

Butterfly farm
Reflections

1. List the characteristics of an insect. (Include the three body parts.)

   _____

   _____

   _____

2. Which part of this activity did you enjoy most? Give a reason for your answer.

   _____

   _____

   _____

3. List three techniques you used to create your Butterfly farm picture.

   _____

   _____

   _____

4. Would younger children find this art project difficult? | Yes | No |
   Give a reason for your answer.

   _____

   _____

   _____

5. Butterfly farms provide a comfortable environment/habitat for the butterflies to live in and breed. Draw/Design a butterfly enclosure, including three things which would ensure the butterflies live comfortably and safely. Label these. Colour your drawing with pencils.

R.I.C. Publications/Prim-Ed Publishing

Butterfly farm
Task assessment

Activity objectives

Arts ideas: *Creates artworks to express ideas.*

Arts skills and processes: *Uses a range of visual arts skills, techniques, procedures, practices and technologies.*

Arts responses: *Uses an aesthetic understanding to acknowledge, reflect on and assess the arts.*

Arts in society: *Demonstrates an understanding of the part that the arts play in society.*

Task

The students were instructed to make a 3-D picture of a scene in a butterfly farm using a range of skills, techniques, mediums and materials.

Assessment key			
✔ **yes** (has demonstrated achievement of this criterion)			
✗ **no** (has not demonstrated achievement of this criterion)			
● **inconsistent** (some evidence of achievement has been shown)			
Criterion			
The student is able to:	✔	✗	●
participate in discussion about insects, butterflies and their environment/habitat.			
draw and colour with strong, solid colour using oil pastels.			
smudge oil pastel colouring to create a blended colour effect.			
paint background using dye.			
make a butterfly template.			
trace a butterfly template to make five butterfly shapes.			
cut out leaf and butterfly shapes accurately using scissors.			
arrange and glue leaf and butterfly shapes onto background.			
add detail to picture using fine permanent black marker.			
complete a reflection sheet based on his/her artwork.			
listen to and follow instructions.			
work cooperatively in an informal activity-based work environment.			

Arbitrary printing

This lesson focuses on developing a colouring technique which may be used for future activities. The process encourages students to experiment with paint, colour and printing with arbitrary tools. Simple printing techniques may be used to make wrapping paper by using a cheap grade of paper.

Two-lesson project

Discussion points

A poster of the colour wheel showing primary, secondary and tertiary colours is useful to inspire meaningful discussion.

- Which colours are the primary colours? (red, blue and yellow)
- Which colours are the secondary colours? (orange, green, purple)
- Which colours are the tertiary colours? (a mixture of primary and secondary colours: red-orange, yellow-orange, yellow, green, blue-green, blue-purple, red-purple.)
- Printing of paint may be completed in many ways. Can you name some of these? (screen printing using a frame and stencil to print an image onto fabric, paper etc.; stencilling, using a sponge and template; direct stamping of objects into paint and then onto desired area etc.)

Template printing is often used where large area markings are essential; e.g. car parks, road markings, sport courts, logos for advertising etc. Spray painting over the template is also often used in large areas.

Paint may also be printed using small arbitrary tools. Demonstrate dipping the edge of a piece of scrap cardboard and dragging the paint to make squares (as shown in first painting of example). Scrape different colours over half the squares. Use bottle top caps/lids to print circles. Fold card to print arrow like shapes.

The number of possible techniques is endless. Encourage students to experiment with colour and different ways to print with it.

- What objects could we use to make different printing effects? (glue stick lid, pen lid, edge of a small cardboard box etc.)

Lesson one

Materials

- ★ cardboard scraps to be cut into small shapes for scraping (approximately 5 cm x 5 cm)
- any arbitrary tools which may be used for printing; e.g. flat-ended pencil, pen lid, glue stick lids
- newspaper to protect workspace
- card for mounting
- black card for mounting
- craft glue for mounting
- scrap recycled paper
- A5 cartridge paper (four sheets per child)

- acrylic paint (variety of colours)
- polystyrene trays (for paint)

Method

1. Following discussion about printing with paint and arbitrary tools and demonstration of basic scraping and printing techniques, encourage students to experiment with printing techniques and various colour combinations on scrap paper. Emphasise making and trying different-sized cardboard tools for scraping.

2. When satisfied with the results, students print four different designs/patterns onto A5 paper. Set aside to dry.

★ 3. Enlist adult assistance to mount work onto black, then coloured card.

Lesson two ○

Materials

- reflection and assessment photocopies
- lead pencil
- coloured pencils

Method

1. Students complete reflection activity.
2. Teacher completes assessment record.

R.I.C. Publications/Prim-Ed Publishing

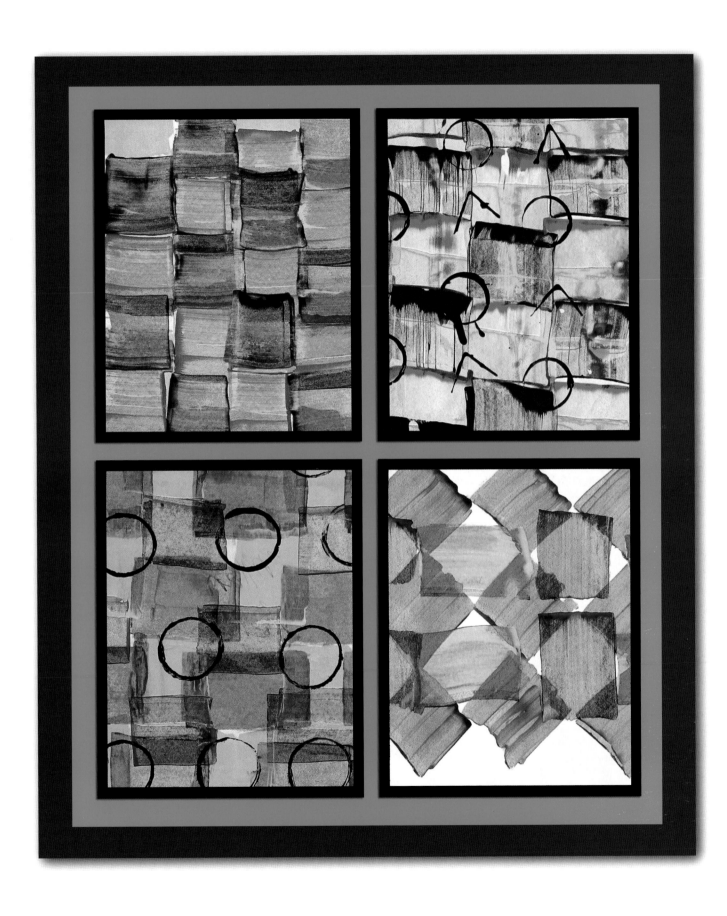

Arbitrary printing
Reflections

1. List three colours for each category.

    Primary: _____

    Secondary: _____

    Tertiary: _____

    _____

2. Which part of this activity did you enjoy most? Give a reason for your answer.

    _____

    _____

3. Were you satisfied with the result you achieved by scraping paint to create patterns?

Yes	No

    Give a reason for your answer.

    _____

    _____

4. Write instructions for someone to make your favourite arbitrary tools pattern. Include a coloured picture to demonstrate the result.

    _____

    _____

    _____

    _____

    _____

    _____

    _____

    _____

    _____

    _____

    _____

R.I.C. Publications/Prim-Ed Publishing

Task assessment

Activity objectives

Arts ideas: *Creates artworks to express ideas.*

Arts skills and processes: *Uses a range of visual arts skills, techniques, procedures, practices and technologies.*

Arts responses: *Uses an aesthetic understanding to acknowledge, reflect on and assess the arts.*

Arts in society: *Demonstrates an understanding of the part that the arts play in society.*

Task

The students were instructed to print a range of patterns using a variety of arbitrary tools, techniques and paint.

Assessment key			
✔ **yes** *(has demonstrated achievement of this criterion)*			
✘ **no** *(has not demonstrated achievement of this criterion)*			
● **inconsistent** *(some evidence of achievement has been shown)*			
Criterion			
The student is able to:	✔	✘	●
participate in discussion about colours and methods of printing with paint using arbitrary tools.			
experiment with arbitrary tools to print paint.			
scrape paint with card.			
print using paint and arbitrary tools.			
complete four different patterns/colour combinations using arbitrary tools.			
complete a reflection sheet based on his/her artwork.			
listen to and follow instructions.			
work cooperatively in an informal activity-based work environment.			

Corrugated card tropical fish

This project was inspired by the theme *The sea*. It incorporates an environmental message to help protect our sea life from extinction. Due to the small size of this project, it has been used as a decorative picture for a greeting card.

Two-lesson project

Discussion points

Stimulus pictures of colourful tropical fish would promote discussion.

- What have you noticed about the colours of tropical fish?
- Why do you think tropical fish have bright colours? (camouflage to live among bright coral etc.)
- What is a habitat? (the natural environment of a plant or animal etc.)
- Lots of people enjoy looking at tropical fish and popular reefs, which are the habitat for beautiful fish, are being spoiled by humans. What can we do to prevent the sea environment from being spoiled? (don't leave rubbish when we go to the beach; when boating, make sure no rubbish goes overboard etc.)

When we visit areas to go snorkelling or reef walking, we must obey the rules which help protect the sea life.

People can keep small tropical fish in aquariums to admire in their homes and workplaces.

Saltwater, and more commonly freshwater, aquariums are available. Some students may have aquariums at home. If so, encourage them to draw their own fish.

Lesson one

★ *Enlist adult assistance to mount card prior to lesson.*

Materials

- A5 photocopy paper
- ★ blue corrugated card (13 cm x 8.5 cm)
- ★ black card (15 cm x 10.5 cm) and (21 cm x 30 cm folded for card)
- ★ purple card (17 cm x 12.5 cm)
- corrugated card in a variety of colours (offcuts are suitable for this project)
- ★ sandpaper (approx. 2 cm x 13 cm)
- small shells (if these aren't available, a mixed bean soup mix is a grainy, effective substitute)
- lead pencil
- scissors
- goggle eyes (8–10 mm in size)
- craft glue for mounting
- newspaper to protect workspace

Method

1. Following discussion about tropical fish and their habitat, encourage children to demonstrate different ways to draw fish and weed on the board.
2. Using lead pencil, students draw a plan for a scene on A5 paper, including sandpaper seabed.

3. When satisfied with scene, students commence making corrugated fish scene. Emphasise that when drawing shapes onto the back of corrugated card, fish will be facing the opposite way to when they are cut out.
4. Students draw and cut out all shapes to compile their picture.
5. Using craft glue, attach pieces and goggle eyes into position on blue corrugated card, blue small shells or soup mix. Apply pressure while drying. An exercise book on top works well.

Lesson two

Materials

- artwork in progress
- craft glue 250 mL (squeeze bottle)
- silver glitter
- reflection and assessment photocopies
- lead pencil
- coloured pencils

Method

1. Squeeze blobs of glue and sprinkle with glitter to make bubbles.
2. Students complete reflection activity.
3. Teacher completes assessment record.

Corrugated card tropical fish

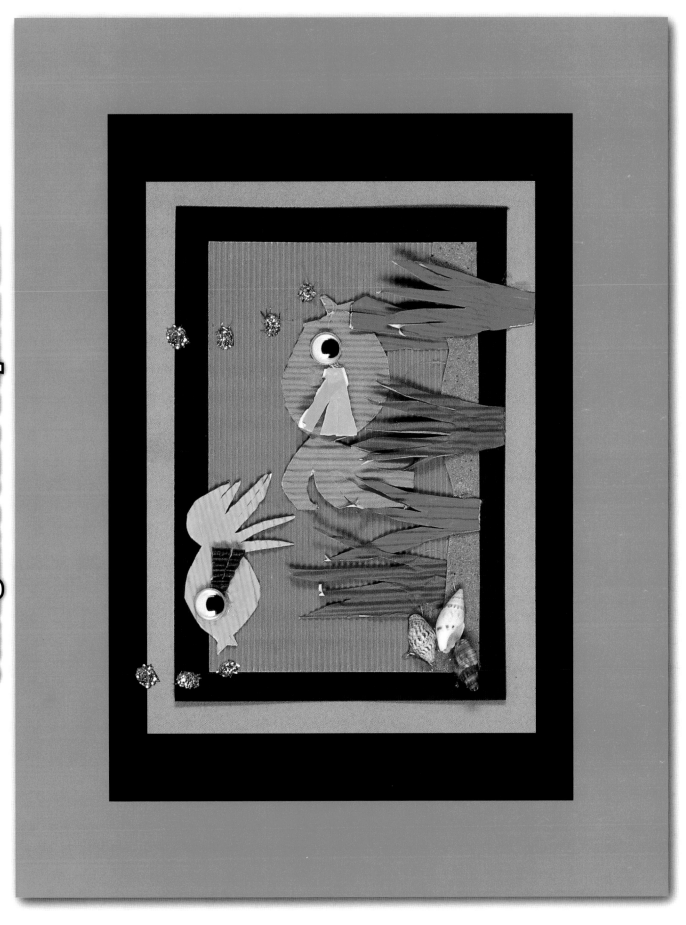

Corrugated card tropical fish
Reflections

1. What is a habitat? _____

   _____

2. Why do you think tropical fish have bright colours?

   _____

   _____

3. List two things we can do to help prevent tropical fish from becoming extinct.

   _____

   _____

4. Which part of this activity did you enjoy most? Give a reason for your answer.

   _____

   _____

   _____

5. Who do you know who would like to receive a greeting card decorated with this design? Give a reason for your answer.

   _____

   _____

6. A similar scene may be effectively used to decorate giftware. Design an item of giftware which could look especially effective decorated with a similar design. Colour your drawing with pencils.

Corrugated card tropical fish
Task assessment

Activity objectives

Arts ideas: *Creates artworks to express ideas.*

Arts skills and processes: *Uses a range of visual arts skills, techniques, procedures, practices and technologies.*

Arts responses: *Uses an aesthetic understanding to acknowledge, reflect on and assess the arts.*

Arts in society: *Demonstrates an understanding of the part that the arts play in society.*

Task

The students were instructed to make a corrugated card fish picture using a
range of skills, techniques and materials.

Assessment key			
✔ **yes** *(has demonstrated achievement of this criterion)*			
✗ **no** *(has not demonstrated achievement of this criterion)*			
● **inconsistent** *(some evidence of achievement has been shown)*			
Criterion			
The student is able to:	✔	✗	●
participate in discussion about tropical fish and caring for the environment.			
draw a plan for a corrugated card fish scene.			
draw fish and weed shapes onto corrugated card from a design drawn on plan.			
cut accurately with scissors.			
arrange and glue picture parts into position.			
add glitter enhancement and small shells or soup mix.			
complete a reflection sheet based on his/her artwork.			
listen to and follow instructions.			
work cooperatively in an informal activity-based work environment.			

R.I.C. Publications/Prim-Ed Publishing

Terracotta hessian sacks

This clay project involves simple welding and effective use of textures. It makes an excellent gift item, as a container for wrapped sweets or chocolates, and it is also an excellent pencil caddy. The example shown was made as a Father's Day gift.

Two lesson project

Discussion points ○○○

- **What is a sack?** (large bag traditionally made from a cheap, loosely-woven fabric called hessian and more tightly woven cloth (calico); today they are also made from plastic-coated hessian-like material)

Historically, sacks were used to hold many things, including grain, flour, sugar, other food products, fertiliser, garden products, livestock food, salt etc.

Sacks were cheap, strong and often reusable. They were filled to the limit and stitched to hold goods inside.

They are still used today to carry bulk quantities of dry items.

Traditionally, Father Christmas carried toys in a sack.

Lesson one ○○

Materials

- arbitrary clay modelling tools, including:
  - ~ conduit rolling pin
  - ~ toothbrush
  - ~ large nail
  - ~ craft stick
  - ~ drinking straw
- polystyrene tray (to contain a small amount of water and a small blob of clay to mix to a thick, creamy, muddy consistency known as 'slurry')
- terracotta clay (approximately fist size)
- ★ hessian cloth pieces (approx. 27 cm x 36 cm)
- newspaper to protect workspace

Method

1. Following discussion about sacks and their purposes, students place clay on top of hessian and, using rolling pin, roll clay to approximately 20 cm wide and 30 cm long. This does not need to be a perfect rectangle; curved, uneven edges create a natural, more rustic effect.
2. Trim edges using a craft stick and a cutting action.
3. Gently score the side edges of the clay with the pointy end of a large nail. Use toothbrush to add a small amount of slurry to assist the joining process.
4. Gently lift the narrow ends together, pressing the long edges to meet in the middle. Mould edges together, leaving about 4 cm at the top. Joining the clay this way is known as 'welding'.
5. Fold the edges back (as shown in example).
6. Using leftover rolled clay, cut three slim leaf shapes and add detail by drawing using the sharp end of a nail.
7. Roll three small round balls to make nuts.

8. Position leaves and nuts onto one side of the sack.
9. Remove leaves and gently score the area where they will be positioned. Score the back of leaves and underneath nuts. Add a small amount of slurry to all joining surfaces using a toothbrush.
10. Gently press and mould leaves and nuts into position using fingers and/or the edge of a craft stick.
11. Make holes in nuts by gently twisting a straw into the surface. Set aside to air dry for a week.
12. Fire according to firing instructions.

Lesson two ○

Materials

- reflection and assessment photocopies
- lead pencil
- coloured pencils

Method

1. Students complete reflection activity.
2. Teacher completes assessment record.

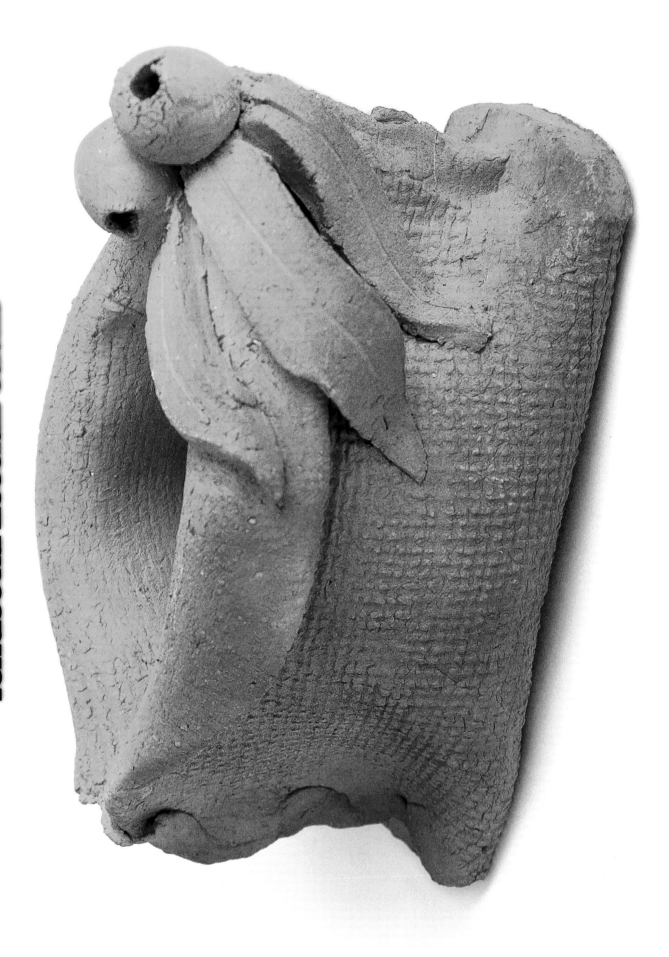

Terracotta hessian sacks

Terracotta hessian sacks
Reflections

1. Sacks have been a useful storage item throughout history. List five items which may be stored in sacks.

_____

_____

2. List five tools you used to make your terracotta sack.

_____

_____

3. Why is it important to score and apply slurry to edges being joined?

_____

_____

4. Were you satisfied with your finished terracotta sack?

Yes	No

Give a reason for your answer and changes you might make next time.

_____

_____

_____

5. Using lead pencil, draw an open sack filled with something of your choice. Colour your drawing with pencils.

Terracotta hessian sacks
Task assessment

Activity objectives

Arts ideas: *Creates artworks to express ideas.*

Arts skills and processes: *Uses a range of visual arts skills, techniques, procedures, practices and technologies.*

Arts responses: *Uses an aesthetic understanding to acknowledge, reflect on and assess the arts.*

Arts in society: *Demonstrates an understanding of the part that the arts play in society.*

Task

The students were instructed to make a terracotta hessian sack using arbitrary tools, terracotta clay and a range of clay modelling techniques.

Assessment key			
✔ **yes** (has demonstrated achievement of this criterion)			
✗ **no** (has not demonstrated achievement of this criterion)			
● **inconsistent** (some evidence of achievement has been shown)			
Criterion			
The student is able to:	✔	✗	●
participate in discussion about sacks and their uses.			
roll clay evenly to approximately 1 cm in thickness.			
roll clay to appropriate size and shape.			
join/weld edges of clay by scoring, using slurry and moulding them together.			
create and make leaves with detail using an arbitrary tool.			
add leaves and nuts by scoring, using slurry and moulding sides/edges together.			
add detail to leaves and nuts using arbitrary tools.			
complete a reflection sheet based on his/her artwork.			
listen to and follow instructions.			
work cooperatively in an informal activity-based work environment.			

Me: A star

This project was inspired by the theme *Music*. The students had been studying different music styles. This art piece followed a TV series promoting and sponsoring young talented people to become stars.

Three-lesson project

Discussion points

- What is a pop star? (a star who performs music which is currently a hit)
- What does a pop singer do? (He or she sings popular songs with backing music. A pop star usually performs with a band and the music is typically suited to dancing with movements.)
- Who is your favourite pop star? (Answers will vary according to personal taste.)
- What style of clothing does your pop star wear? (List items on the board.)
- If a pop star wanted to be noticed, what sort of clothing might he/she wear? (glitz and glamour to attract attention)
- Discuss the job description of pop stars. What is their role in society? (entertain people; provide music to dance and sing along with)
- Why is it important for a pop star to be a good role model for young people? (young people imitate their idols; they have a responsibility to their public audience etc.)
- Imagine you are a pop star. What would you wear? How could you wear your hair? Would you wear accessories? Which songs would you sing? Encourage students to imagine how they would like to look if they were a pop star.

Lesson one

Materials

- A3 cartridge paper
- A4 cartridge paper
- lead pencil/eraser
- thick permanent black marker
- wax crayons
- newspaper to protect workspace

Method

1. Following discussion about pop stars and their appearance if they were a pop star, students use lead pencil to draw themselves as a pop star on A4 paper. Include desired effects to be achieved; e.g. texture rubbing and painting with dye. Include spotlights and, in the foreground, the child's name. This is the plan for the project.
2. When satisfied with drawing, students transfer drawing to A3 cartridge paper in portrait position.
3. Erase unwanted lines.
4. Using permanent black marker, trace over pencil lines.

5. Using wax crayon, colour spotlight area using a texture rubbing technique. (Rubbing crayon over page while leaning on a textured surface; e.g. concrete or brick paving.)

Lesson two

Materials

- artwork in progress
- wax crayons and/or oil pastels
- Edicol™ dye in a variety of colours
- card for mounting
- craft glue for mounting
- paintbrush (medium)
- newspaper to protect workspace

Method

1. Complete colouring picture using wax crayons and/or oil pastels.
2. Using a medium paintbrush, paint over textured crayon if rubbing, (light beams) and background using dye. Set aside to dry.
★ 3. Enlist adult help to mount work onto coloured card.

Lesson three

Materials

- artwork in progress
- craft glue for mounting
- paintbrush (fine)
- glitter (variety of colours)
- newspaper to protect workspace
- reflection and assessment photocopies
- lead pencil
- coloured pencils

Method

1. Using fine brush, paint craft glue over name and sprinkle with glitter. Set aside to dry.
2. Students complete reflection activity.
3. Teacher completes assessment record.

Me: A star

Me: A star
Reflections

1. Which part of this activity did you enjoy most? Give a reason for your answer.

   _____

   _____

   _____

2. List six tools, mediums and materials you used to make your picture.

   _____

   _____

   _____

3. Write numbered instructions for a texture rubbing background painted with dye.

   _____

   _____

   _____

4. Why is it important for pop stars to be good role models?

   _____

   _____

5. List three songs you would like to sing if you were a famous pop star.

   _____

   _____

   _____

6. Using lead pencil, draw a cover for your first number one CD. To colour your design, include three different colouring techniques. Label your design to show where each is used.

R.I.C. Publications/Prim-Ed Publishing

Task assessment

Activity objectives

Arts ideas: *Creates artworks to express ideas.*

Arts skills and processes: *Uses a range of visual arts skills, techniques, procedures, practices and technologies.*

Arts responses: *Uses an aesthetic understanding to acknowledge, reflect on and assess the arts.*

Arts in society: *Demonstrates an understanding of the part that the arts play in society.*

Task

The students were instructed to make a picture of themselves as a pop star performing, using a range of skills, techniques and materials.

Assessment key			
✔ **yes** (has demonstrated achievement of this criterion)			
✘ **no** (has not demonstrated achievement of this criterion)			
● **inconsistent** (some evidence of achievement has been shown)			
Criterion			
The student is able to:	✔	✘	●
participate in discussion about pop stars and songs/music.			
draw a picture of himself/herself as a pop star, using lead pencil.			
trace his/her drawing using permanent black marker.			
add stage features to drawing.			
make a texture rubbing using wax crayon.			
demonstrate solid colouring using wax crayons and/or oil pastels.			
paint over wax crayon rubbing and background with dye.			
enhance picture with glitter highlights.			
complete a reflection sheet based on his/her artwork.			
listen to and follow instructions.			
work cooperatively in an informal activity-based work environment.			

Mystical mermaid/merman

This project was inspired by the theme *The sea*. Myths and legends of the sea, including mermaids, were incorporated into the language areas of writing and reading.

Discussion points

- What is a mermaid? (an imaginary female sea creature with a human-like upper body and fish lower body)
- Because mermaids are fantasy creatures, we can make them into anything we wish; e.g. glitzy, reptilian etc.
- Do you know any famous mermaids in books or movies? (Answers will vary from animated to more realistic movies and books.)
- Although mermaids are imaginary, because they are human-like, what might they need to survive? (air, food, water) Think about what a mermaid might eat. List ideas on the board.
- What would a merman look like? Some students may prefer to develop an imaginary half-human, half-fish male sea creature.
- Describe when you might find a merman/mermaid (its habitat).

Lesson one

Materials

- cartridge paper (56 cm x 36 cm)
- wax crayons (yellow)
- Edicol™ dye (bright blue and yellow)
- paintbrush (thick)
- A3 photocopy paper
- ★ prepared mermaid/merman template (page 134)
- lead pencil
- card for mounting
- craft glue for mounting
- newspaper to protect workspace

Method

1. Following discussion, students use yellow wax crayon to draw a sand line across bottom of cartridge paper and colour with strong, solid colour.
2. Using blue dye, paint the remainder of the page. Page must be very wet. Use brush to drop yellow dye along the edge of sand line. Hold picture upside down so that yellow dye can run down the page to represent seaweed. Set aside to dry.
3. Trace mermaid/merman template onto A3 photocopy paper.
4. Plan the appearance of your sea creature. Label your ideas to show the

Four-lesson project

colouring technique you will use for each section.

★ 5. Enlist adult assistance to mount background onto coloured card before Lesson two.

Lesson two

Materials

- artwork in progress
- soup mix
- small shells (optional)
- prepared mermaid/merman template
- oil pastels
- wrapping paper (brightly coloured) (recycled is suitable)
- recycled cardboard (cereal box works well)
- egg cartons
- cartridge paper A3
- lead pencil
- permanent black marker
- scissors
- glue stick
- craft glue 250 mL (squeeze bottle)
- newspaper to protect workspace

Method

1. Drizzle craft glue randomly over sand section of picture.
2. Sprinkle with soup mix. If available, press small shells into position.
3. Cut egg carton cups roughly.
4. Glue in position on background using craft glue generously. Set aside to dry.
5. Using template and lead pencil, trace mermaid/merman shape onto A3 cartridge paper.
6. Using lead pencil, lightly draw facial features.
7. Colour trunk and face using oil pastels.
8. Trace facial feature outlines with fine permanent black marker.
9. Using glue stick, glue onto cardboard to give extra strength. Cut around outline.
10. Cut sections of mermaid/merman plan as templates for remainder of picture.
11. Using glue stick, glue tail shape wrapping paper onto mermaid.
12. Make mermaid's bikini top by gluing small shells into position with craft glue or making shapes with wrapping paper and fastening using glue stick. Set aside to dry.

Lesson three

Materials

- artwork in progress
- craft glue for mounting

- silver glitter
- paintbrushes (fine and medium)
- brown acrylic paint
- polystyrene trays (for paint)
- scissors
- newspaper to protect workspace
- wool
- recycled cardboard

Method

1. To add glitter detail to mermaid/ merman, paint craft glue onto required area and sprinkle with glitter.
2. Paint bubbles onto background and sprinkle with silver glitter.
3. To make hair, wind wool around a piece of card double the width of the length of hair required. Tie a piece of wool around the hair at one end of the piece of card. Cut the hair along the other end of card.
4. Glue to mermaid/merman's head using craft glue. Set aside to dry.
5. Carefully paint egg carton rocks and set aside to dry.

Lesson four

Materials

- artwork in progress
- cork (from a wine bottle)
- scissors
- hot glue gun
- tissue paper (green tones)
- glue stick
- newspaper to protect workspace
- reflection and assessment photocopies
- lead pencil
- coloured pencils

Method

1. Using hot glue gun, fasten cork to back of head.
★ 2. Glue mermaid/merman onto background using hot glue gun.
3. Cut tissue paper lengths approximately 3 cm x 30 cm and twist together to make seaweed.
4. Arrange seaweed and, using glue stick generously, glue into position. Set aside to dry.
5. Students complete reflection activity.
6. Teacher completes assessment record.

Name: _____   Date: _____

Mystical mermaid/merman
Reflections

1. List eight materials, mediums and tools you used to make your scene.

_____
_____
_____

2. Which part of this activity did you enjoy most? Give a reason for your answer.

_____
_____
_____

3. Which technique did you find most difficult while making your Mystical mermaid/ merman scene? Give a reason for your answer.

_____
_____
_____

4. What is a habitat? _____

_____

5. List the three necessities for humans to survive.

_____ _____ _____

6. Mermaids/Mermen are fictitious. Draw another fictitious sea creature. Colour your drawing using pencils.

[ ]

68 | *Primary art*

R.I.C. Publications/Prim-Ed Publishing

Mystical mermaid/merman
Task assessment

Activity objectives

Arts ideas: *Creates artworks to express ideas.*

Arts skills and processes: *Uses a range of visual arts skills, techniques, procedures, practices and technologies.*

Arts responses: *Uses an aesthetic understanding to acknowledge, reflect on and assess the arts.*

Arts in society: *Demonstrates an understanding of the part that the arts play in society.*

Task

The students were instructed to make a mystical mermaid/merman picture using a range of skills, techniques, mediums and materials.

Assessment key			
✔ **yes** (has demonstrated achievement of this criterion)			
✗ **no** (has not demonstrated achievement of this criterion)			
● **inconsistent** (some evidence of achievement has been shown)			
Criterion			
The student is able to:	✔	✗	●
participate in discussion about mermaids, imaginary sea creatures, habitats and human needs.			
demonstrate solid colouring using wax crayons and oil pastels.			
paint using dye.			
add detail to sand by drizzling craft glue and sprinkling with soup mix.			
demonstrate tracing a prepared shape.			
make a pattern for tracing.			
cut accurately using scissors.			
twist tissue paper.			
complete a picture using the specified techniques.			
add glitter enhancement.			
complete a reflection sheet based on his/her artwork.			
listen to and follow instructions.			
work cooperatively in an informal activity-based work environment.			

Summer bushfires

This art project was inspired by the theme *Natural disasters*. Uncontrolled bushfires are a major problem for many countries worldwide each summer. Stimulus pictures of fire scenes inspire realistic representation and meaningful discussion.

Two-lesson project

Discussion points ○○○

- What is a bushfire? (a fire in forest or scrub country)
- What conditions make up a high risk for bushfires to occur? (weather—dry spells, heat, wind)
- Do natural bushfires have a positive purpose? (natural culling, rejuvenating plant life)
- What colours are associated with summer and bushfires? (warm colours)
- Are there any high risk areas in your locality? (Answers will vary.)
- How can we prevent bushfires from occurring? (fire prevention: keep sites free of rubbish and dead vegetation, firebreaks, adhering to fire prevention practices etc.)
- What causes fire? (natural causes, including lightning strikes; human causes, including arson or carelessness.)

Unfortunately, there are dangerous people in society who actually start fires with the intention of causing destruction. These people are known as firebugs or arsonists.

Trained firefighters risk their lives to put out fires which threaten the property and lives of innocent people. Unfortunately, many lives have been lost through fires caused by natural causes, the carelessness of others or which have been lit intentionally.

- How can we create depth/distance in our painting? (by decreasing the size of detail in the background)

  Demonstrate this by drawing a simple scene on the board, with trees decreasing in size.

  Demonstrate gradual colour blending. Emphasise the need to add dark to light colour in very small amounts.

Lesson one ○○

Materials

- 2 sheets of A3 cartridge paper per child
- paintbrush (medium)
- yellow, red and black acrylic paint
- cardboard offcuts
- polystyrene trays (for paint)
- card for mounting
- craft glue for mounting
- newspaper to protect workspace
- black paint

Method

1. Following discussion about bushfires, line up two sheets of A3 cartridge paper in portrait position.
2. Starting with yellow paint, brush from side-to-side with long, fluent strokes across both sheets of paper at tops of pages. Add a small amount of red paint and paint next section down. Gradually add more red paint while continuing to paint down page to create a gradual colour change from yellow to orange to red. Set aside one piece to dry.
3. Using black paint and paintbrush, paint a tree trunk and main limbs in top two-thirds of one painted sheet.
4. Using cardboard offcuts, print remainder of scene detail. This may be a blackened farmhouse, trees, fencing etc. Emphasise creating depth/distance by decreasing the size of detail in the background. Set aside to dry.
★ 5. Enlist adult assistance to mount blackened scene onto coloured card before Lesson two.

Lesson two ●○○

Materials

- artwork in progress
- lead pencil
- scissors
- glue stick
- newspaper to protect workspace
- reflection and assessment photocopies
- coloured pencils

Method

1. Draw flames on the back of second sheet, as shown below, and cut out.

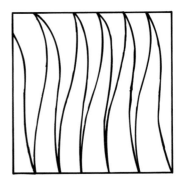

2. Glue flames into place, starting from the bottom of the picture.
3. Create a 3-D effect by securing flames at three points only with glue stick. Entwine flames to enhance reality.
4. Students complete reflection activity.
5. Teacher completes assessment record.

R.I.C. Publications/Prim-Ed Publishing

Summer bushfires

R.I.C. Publications/Prim-Ed Publishing

Summer bushfires
Reflections

1. What is the best way to blend two colours to demonstrate gradual colour change?

_____

_____

_____

2. Were you satisfied with the colour blending? Why/Why not? Give reasons for your answer.

Yes	No

_____

_____

3. What did you include in your design that created depth/distance in your overall picture?

_____

_____

4. List five tools necessary to create this art piece.

_____

_____

5. Which part of this activity did you enjoy most? Give reasons for your answer.

_____

_____

6. Why are arsonists a menace to society? _____

_____

7. Fire can engulf almost anything. Using lead pencil, draw another fire scene. Colour your drawing with pencils.

Summer bushfires
Task assessment

Activity objectives

Arts ideas: *Creates artworks to express ideas.*

Arts skills and processes: *Uses a range of visual arts skills, techniques, procedures, practices and technologies.*

Arts responses: *Uses an aesthetic understanding to acknowledge, reflect on and assess the arts.*

Arts in society: *Demonstrates an understanding of the part that the arts play in society.*

Task

The students were instructed to make a summer bushfire picture using a range of
skills, techniques, mediums and materials.

Assessment key			
✔ **yes** *(has demonstrated achievement of this criterion)*			
✗ **no** *(has not demonstrated achievement of this criterion)*			
● **inconsistent** *(some evidence of achievement has been shown)*			
Criterion			
The student is able to:	✔	✗	●
blend paint colour by mixing dark into light.			
paint a gradual blended colour change.			
demonstrate brush painting.			
paint detail by printing paint with the edge of card.			
demonstrate depth of field through diminishing size.			
draw, cut out and glue flames onto picture, creating a 3-D effect.			
complete a reflection sheet based on his/her artwork.			
listen to and follow instructions.			
work cooperatively in an informal activity-based work environment.			

Primary art **73**

Terrific tourist T-shirt

This project was inspired by a news-telling session following a holiday period. Several students brought in souvenirs, including a cap and T-shirt, when telling about their holiday experiences. Class discussion followed about promoting tourist attractions using souvenirs with logos, slogans, greetings typical to a place/country etc.

Three-lesson project

Discussion points

- Where is your favourite holiday destination? (Answers will vary according to personal choice.)
- What tourist attractions are promoted at this place?
- What methods of advertising are used to promote a tourist destination? (pamphlets, brochures, clothing—hats, caps—radio and television advertisements, word of mouth etc.)
- Why would clothing advertising be effective? (it is mobile; people may ask the wearer about the destination and the wearer will promote it by word of mouth)

Showing snapshots of tourist attractions will initiate more design ideas.

Lesson one

Materials

- T-shirt shape on photocopy paper (page 135)
- T-shirt shape on A3 cartridge paper (photocopy)
- lead pencil/eraser
- thick permanent black marker
- fine permanent black marker
- oil pastels—standard and fluorescent
- newspaper to protect workspace

Method

1. Following discussion about favourite holiday destinations, tourist attractions and advertising, students use lead pencil to draw a plan of a T-shirt onto photocopy showing 'snapshots' of a favourite holiday destination—or somewhere they might like to visit for a holiday.

    Indicate colours to be used by colouring small sections of each design.

2. When satisfied with results, students use lead pencil to transfer design to cartridge paper T-shirt shape.

3. Trace pencil lines with permanent black marker and fine liner.

4. Students colour design using oil pastels and strong, solid colour.

Lesson two

Materials

- artwork in progress
- oil pastels—standard or fluorescent
- newspaper to protect workspace
- scissors

Method

1. Complete colouring T-shirt design.
2. Cut out completed design.

Lesson three

Materials

- artwork in progress
- newspaper to protect workspace
- glue stick
- craft glue for mounting
- 2 clothes pegs per child
- coloured card
- paintbrush (fine)
- silver glitter
- reflection and assessment photocopies
- lead pencil
- coloured pencils

Method

1. Using glue stick, glue T-shirt into position on coloured card, leaving top edge unglued.

2. Using craft glue and fine paintbrush, paint a clothes line as shown in example.

3. Sprinkle with silver glitter.

4. Peg edges of T-shirt and, using craft glue, glue pegs into position. Set aside to dry.

5. Students complete reflection activity.

6. Teacher completes assessment record.

Terrific tourist T-shirt

Terrific tourist T-shirt
Reflections

1. What place did you choose to promote using your T-shirt design?

   _____

2. List the tourist attractions you included in your design.

   _____

   _____

3. Which is your favourite tourist attraction? Why? _____

   _____

   _____

4. Which part of this activity did you enjoy most? Give a reason for your answer.

   _____

   _____

5. Why do you think your T-shirt design will be an effective tourist promotion?

   _____

   _____

6. Were you satisfied with the finished effect? Give a reason for your answer.

Yes	No

   _____

   _____

7. Caps and hats may also be effective to promote tourist attractions. Draw a design, promoting a theme park tourist attraction, suitable for the front of a cap/hat. Colour your design using pencils.

R.I.C. Publications/Prim-Ed Publishing

Terrific tourist T-shirt
Task assessment

Activity objectives

Arts ideas: *Creates artworks to express ideas.*

Arts skills and processes: *Uses a range of visual arts skills, techniques, procedures, practices and technologies.*

Arts responses: *Uses an aesthetic understanding to acknowledge, reflect on and assess the arts.*

Arts in society: *Demonstrates an understanding of the part that the arts play in society.*

Task

The students were instructed to design a promotional T-shirt, using a range
of skills, techniques, mediums and materials.

Assessment key			
✔ **yes** *(has demonstrated achievement of this criterion)*			
✗ **no** *(has not demonstrated achievement of this criterion)*			
● **inconsistent** *(some evidence of achievement has been shown)*			
Criterion			
The student is able to:	✔	✗	●
participate in discussion about favourite holiday destinations, tourist attractions and advertising.			
draw a plan for a promotional design on a T-shirt.			
transfer the design onto a T-shirt shape on cartridge paper.			
draw over pencil lines using thick and fine permanent black markers.			
demonstrate strong, solid colouring using oil pastels.			
complete a reflection sheet based on his/her artwork.			
listen to and follow instructions.			
work cooperatively in an informal activity-based work environment.			

Torn paper 'sun and sea'

This project was inspired by the topic *Sun and sea*, as part of the theme, *The seasons.* The pleasures of each season's weather characteristics were discussed, including summer sunsets at the beach (on the west coast) or over the land (east coast). Recycling of an assortment of paper scraps makes this activity environmentally friendly, encouraging the students to use 'waste' paper.

Three-lesson project

Discussion points

A colour wheel showing primary, secondary and tertiary colours will enhance meaningful discussion.

- What are the characteristics of summer weather? (Answers will vary depending on locality: warm, hot, dry conditions.)
- Which are the warm colours? Refer to colour wheel. (reds, oranges, yellows, browns etc.)
- Which colours are the cool colours? Refer to colour wheel. (blues, greens, purples)
- Which category of colours would you choose to make the sun? (warm colours)
- What is recycling? (reusing products, especially natural resources, by repeated use or reprocessing)
- What can we do to recycle at home? (ensure that we correctly dispose of recyclable materials; e.g. recycling bins and outlets; wherever possible, return organic material to the earth; e.g. turning vegetable matter into compost; avoid wasting paper etc.)

Reusing paper products to make art projects can be a very effective example of recycling.

Lesson one

Materials

- A3 cartridge paper
- scrap paper: warm and cool colours:
  – metallic paper
  – plain coloured paper
  – metallic crepe paper
  – tissue paper
- glue stick
- newspaper to protect workspace

Method

1. Following discussion about summer, warm and cool colours and recycling, students tear an assortment of paper into long, thin strips. Loosely fold cartridge paper in half, width wise, in portrait position.

2. Students glue warm colour paper strips into a sun ray formation on the top half of the page. Emphasise gluing down the edges and covering the whole section of the page.

3. Tear red and gold metallic paper into small pieces for the sun.

4. Glue sun formation onto the page.

5. Tear cool coloured paper into long thin strips for the sea.

6. Glue into position.

Lesson two

Materials

- artwork in progress
- materials required to complete Lesson one
- newspaper to protect workspace
- scissors/slide trimmer
- coloured card for mounting
- craft glue for mounting

Method

1. Complete torn paper sun and sea design.

★ 2. Enlist adult assistance to trim and mount work onto coloured card.

Lesson three

Materials

- reflection and assessment photocopies
- lead pencil
- coloured pencils

Method

1. Students complete reflection activity.

2. Teacher completes assessment record.

Torn paper 'sun and sea'

Torn paper 'sun and sea'
Reflections

1. Write three favourable characteristics of summer.

   _____

   _____

   _____

2. List four warm colours.

   _____   _____   _____   _____

3. List four cool colours.

   _____   _____   _____   _____

4. Which part of this activity did you enjoy most? Give a reason for your answer.

   _____

   _____

5. Were you satisfied with the finished effect?
   Give a reason for your answer.

Yes	No

   _____

   _____

6. What is recycling? _____

   _____

7. Why is it important to recycle? _____

   _____

8. Summer is associated with warm weather. Using lead pencil, draw yourself participating in a summer-related beach activity. Colour your design using pencils.

R.I.C. Publications/Prim-Ed Publishing

Torn paper 'sun and sea'
Task assessment

Activity objectives

Arts ideas: *Creates artworks to express ideas.*

Arts skills and processes: *Uses a range of visual arts skills, techniques, procedures, practices and technologies.*

Arts responses: *Uses an aesthetic understanding to acknowledge, reflect on and assess the arts.*

Arts in society: *Demonstrates an understanding of the part that the arts play in society.*

Task

The students were instructed to make a torn paper representation of the sea and sun using a range of skills, techniques, mediums and materials.

Assessment key
✔ **yes** *(has demonstrated achievement of this criterion)*
✗ **no** *(has not demonstrated achievement of this criterion)*
● **inconsistent** *(some evidence of achievement has been shown)*

Criterion			
The student is able to:	✔	✗	●
participate in discussion about summer, warm and cool colours and recycling.			
tear paper into long, thin strips.			
tear paper into small pieces.			
glue torn paper into position to make a paper representation of the sea and the sun.			
complete a reflection sheet based on his/her artwork.			
listen to and follow instructions.			
work cooperatively in an informal activity-based work environment.			

City reflections

This art project was inspired by a classroom calendar featuring Monet's artwork. The activity allows students to experiment with the use of stencils, sponge painting and creating a soft, slightly blurred effect using a finger painting technique.

Two-lesson project

Discussion points

Stimulus pictures of Monet paintings as examples of soft/blurred effect and a colour wheel showing primary, secondary and tertiary colours will enhance meaningful discussion. Monet's paintings are often available as a set of calendar pictures.

- Where have you seen a building reflected in water? (Answers will vary: city buildings reflected in the river, port buildings reflected in waterways, boathouses reflected in the river etc.)
- Is the reflection as vivid/clear as the actual objects being reflected? Discuss the softening of lines due to the nature of the water surface.
- Introduce the method of blurring colour using finger painting to achieve a slightly blurred effect, as did Monet. Demonstrate the technique before commencing project if desired.
- Which colours are cool colours? (blues, greens, purples)
- Which colours are warm colours? (red, orange, yellow)

Lesson one

Materials

- A3 cartridge paper
- acrylic paint—variety of colours, including cool colours
- polystyrene trays (for paint)
- sponges
- scissors
- recycled cardboard (A3 length)
- glue stick lid
- lead pencil
- paintbrush (fine)
- card for mounting
- newspaper to protect workspace
- craft glue for mounting

Method

1. Following discussion about Monet's paintings, characteristics of reflections on water and warm and cool colours, students fold A3 cartridge in half lengthwise.
2. Place cardboard over top half of A3 cartridge in landscape position.
3. Using lead pencil, draw a building scape onto cardboard.
4. Using scissors, carefully cut along the pencil lines. These will be your stencils for sponging background. (sky and buildings).

5. Using light tones of blue, finger paint top half of cartridge paper using 'pat and lift' technique. Emphasise no dragging. (around cardboard building shapes.)
6. Using dark tones of blue, finger paint lower half of cartridge paper using 'pat and lift' technique. Emphasise no dragging.
7. Place the sky side of the cardboard stencil onto the top half of the finger painting and using a sponge, paint building shapes onto paper. Use a 'pat and lift' technique. (It doesn't matter if sky is wet – don't apply pressure to card).
8. Cut sponges to size to print rectangular windows. A glue stick lid may be used to print round windows.
9. Finger paint reflection of buildings on lower half of picture, using the same colours.
10. Print windows with a sponge and glue stick lid, moving it slightly to create a blurred effect.
11. Using the end of a paintbrush, draw a line (horizontal) dividing the buildings from the reflections.
12. Using the edge of a piece of recycled cardboard, print streetlights on both sections.
13. Lights can be printed with the end of a brush handle. Set aside to dry.
★ 14. Enlist adult help to mount work onto coloured card (optional).

Lesson two

Materials

- reflection and assessment photocopies
- lead pencil
- coloured pencils

Method

1. Students complete reflection activity.
2. Teacher completes assessment record.

R.I.C. Publications/Prim-Ed Publishing

City reflections
Reflections

1. Which part of this activity did you enjoy most? Give a reason for your answer.

_____

_____

2. Were you able to achieve the blurred colour effect which is the feature of Monet's work?

Yes	No

Describe the technique you used to try to achieve this.

_____

_____

3. If you were to use this technique to build a forest reflection, what colours would you use?

_____

_____

4. How would you achieve tree reflections? Consider techniques you have used in the past.

_____

_____

5. What other scenes have you seen reflected in water?

_____

6. Draw another water reflection you have seen. Colour your drawing with pencils. Give your drawing a title.

Title: _____

R.I.C. Publications/Prim-Ed Publishing

Task assessment

Activity objectives
Arts ideas: *Creates artworks to express ideas.*

Arts skills and processes: *Uses a range of visual arts skills, techniques, procedures, practices and technologies.*

Arts responses: *Uses an aesthetic understanding to acknowledge, reflect on and assess the arts.*

Arts in society: *Demonstrates an understanding of the part that the arts play in society.*

Task
The students were instructed to make a city reflections picture using a range of skills, techniques, mediums and materials.

Assessment key			
✔ **yes** (has demonstrated achievement of this criterion)			
✘ **no** (has not demonstrated achievement of this criterion)			
● **inconsistent** (some evidence of achievement has been shown)			
Criterion			
The student is able to:	✔	✘	●
participate in class discussion about Monet and reflections.			
draw and make a stencil for a city scape.			
cut accurately along dotted line.			
demonstrate finger painting using 'pat and lift' technique.			
demonstrate sponging using 'pat and lift' technique.			
print using the edge of card.			
complete making a city scene reflection painting.			
complete a reflection sheet based on his/her artwork.			
listen to and follow instructions.			
work cooperatively in an informal activity-based work environment.			

Spiral eye teaser

This project was inspired by an optical illusion (eye teaser) book a child bought in for a book review. Several students were keen to research impossible drawings. A focus was placed on drawing even curves, using the wrist as an axis/pivot. Prior to the lesson, encourage students to research optical illusions as a homework activity.

Three-lesson project

Discussion points

Optical illusion pictures will inspire meaningful discussion. Encourage students to bring in pictures they have located during research.

- What is an optical illusion? (a false impression of an optical/visual nature)
- What are the characteristics of optical illusion pictures? (When we look at drawings where lines are close together, our eyes are 'teased'. An example of this is when we look at a spiral.

Lesson one

Materials

- recycled photocopy paper (to practise drawing curved lines)
- cartridge paper (29.5 cm x 29.5 cm)
- lead pencil/eraser
- black permanent marker
- coloured permanent markers
- newspaper to protect workspace
- rulers

Method

1. Following discussion about optical illusions (eye teasers), students use lead pencil to practise drawing curves using the wrist as the pivot/axis. It is important to turn the page as you go to continue fluent wrist action. Emphasise keeping distance between lines as even as possible.

2. Using lead pencil, students draw spirals on square cartridge paper.

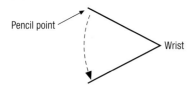

3. Rule a line from corner to corner etc. to make four equal sections, then mid-page to mid page to make eight sections. Finally, halve these sections to make sixteen sections.

4. Using coloured permanent markers, choose six colours and colour in a repetitive pattern from the centre outwards.

Lesson two

Materials

- artwork in progress
- coloured permanent markers
- newspaper to protect workspace
- coloured card for mounting
- craft glue for mounting

Method

1. Complete colouring sectioned spiral with permanent coloured markers.

★ 2. Enlist adult help to mount work onto coloured card.

Lesson three

Materials

- reflection and assessment photocopies
- lead pencil
- coloured pencils

Method

1. Students complete reflection activity.

2. Teacher completes assessment record.

Spiral eye teaser

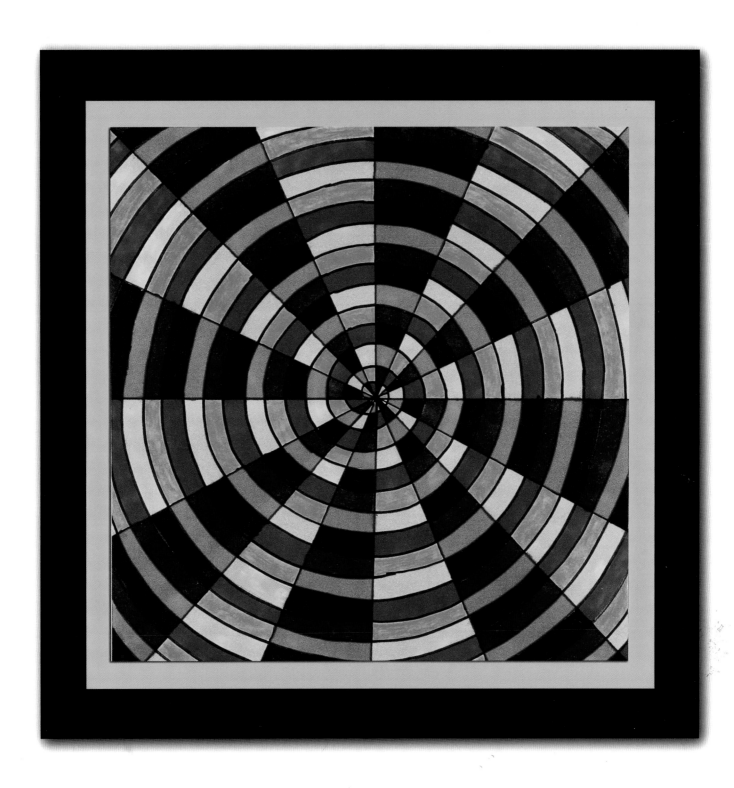

R.I.C. Publications/Prim-Ed Publishing

Spiral eye teaser
Reflections

1. Which part of this activity did you enjoy most? Give a reason for your answer.

_____

_____

2. Which part of this activity was most challenging? Give a reason for your answer.

_____

_____

_____

3. List one characteristic of an optical illusion.

_____

_____

4. List the colours, in order, that you used for your spiral eye teaser.

_____

_____

5. Draw an example of a spiral eye teaser with eight sections and five different colours. What do you notice about the pattern?

_____

_____

6. Using lead pencil, draw a gift item featuring an optical illusion design. Colour your drawing.

Spiral eye teaser
Task assessment

Activity objectives
Arts ideas: *Creates artworks to express ideas.*
Arts skills and processes: *Uses a range of visual arts skills, techniques, procedures, practices and technologies.*
Arts responses: *Uses an aesthetic understanding to acknowledge, reflect on and assess the arts.*
Arts in society: *Demonstrates an understanding of the part that the arts play in society.*

Task
The students were instructed to make a spiral line picture using a range
of skills, techniques, mediums and materials.

Assessment key		
✔ **yes** *(has demonstrated achievement of this criterion)*		
✗ **no** *(has not demonstrated achievement of this criterion)*		
● **inconsistent** *(some evidence of achievement has been shown)*		
Criterion		
The student is able to:	✔	✗	●
participate in discussion about optical illusion.			
draw a spiral using the wrist as an axis/pivot.			
rule straight lines to section spiral drawing.			
colour using a repetitive, colour-based pattern.			
complete a reflection sheet based on his/her artwork.			
listen to and follow instructions.			
work cooperatively in an informal activity-based work environment.			

Sad clown contour drawing

This art project was inspired by an incursion to the school which included clowns. The many faces of the clowns demonstrated a variety of emotions, ranging from very sad through to incredibly happy. The actual activity followed a written lesson focusing on adjectives used in describing a clown. Dramatisation using facial expressions to demonstrate emotions is also appropriate.

The ethics of laughing at another person demonstrating various emotions was also discussed in detail. Photos and pictures of clowns were the basis for this contour drawing activity. Alternatively, a student may dress up as a clown to be the model, varying facial expressions.

Two-lesson project

Discussion points

- What is a clown? (Answers will vary: Record appropriate responses on board; one who amuses others by tricks, odd actions, jokes etc.)
- What do clowns do? (entertain people by making them laugh etc.)
- What do clowns wear? (Outfits range from dull and tatty to bright and colourful. Often clothes are too big, including accessories – nose, shoes, tie etc. List students' ideas on the board.)
- If you were a clown, what sort of tricks or actions would you perform to make people laugh? (Answers will vary.)
- What is a contour drawing? (a continuous drawing, completed using one continuous drawing motion, of the outline of a figure or object.)

Demonstrate drawing a simple contour drawing of an object in the classroom. Allow for looking at the page to check the direction of drawing implement, but mostly only allow looking at the object to be drawn. Emphasise that the drawing implement is not to be lifted off the paper.

Lesson one

Materials

- A3 cartridge paper
- permanent black marker
- craft glue for mounting
- card for mounting (example also included foil board) (optional)

Method

1. Following discussion about clowns and contour drawings, students complete a contour drawing of a clown from either photos/pictures or a model, using permanent black marker on A3 cartridge paper in portrait position.
★ 2. Enlist adult help to mount artwork onto coloured card.

Lesson two

Materials

- *reflection and assessment photocopies*
- *coloured pencils*
- *lead pencils*

Method

1. Students complete reflection activity.
2. Teacher completes assessment record.

Sad clown contour drawing

Sad clown contour drawing
Reflections

1. Clowns perform all kinds of tricks and actions to make people laugh. What kinds of things in a clown's performance make you laugh? Give two examples.

   _____

   _____

2. Clowns display different emotions, ranging from very sad to very happy. Do you think it is wrong to laugh at a clown who is demonstrating very sad emotions? Give a reason for your answer.

   _____

   _____

   _____

3. If you were a clown, would you prefer to wear a bright and colourful or tatty and dull costume? Give a reason for your answer.

   _____

   _____

   _____

4. What is a contour drawing? _____

   _____

5. Were you satisfied with the result of your clown contour drawing? | Yes | No |
   Give a reason for your answer.

   _____

   _____

   _____

6. Using lead pencil, draw a small contour drawing of an object in the classroom. Colour your drawing using pencils.

R.I.C. Publications/Prim-Ed Publishing

Sad clown contour drawing
Task assessment

Activity objectives

Arts ideas: *Creates artworks to express ideas.*

Arts skills and processes: *Uses a range of visual arts skills, techniques, procedures, practices and technologies.*

Arts responses: *Uses an aesthetic understanding to acknowledge, reflect on and assess the arts.*

Arts in society: *Demonstrates an understanding of the part that the arts play in society.*

Task

The students were instructed to complete a contour drawing of a clown, using a range of skills and basic materials.

Assessment key			
✔ **yes** *(has demonstrated achievement of this criterion)*			
✗ **no** *(has not demonstrated achievement of this criterion)*			
● **inconsistent** *(some evidence of achievement has been shown)*			
Criterion			
The student is able to:	✔	✗	●
participate in discussion about clowns and contour drawing.			
complete a contour drawing using a permanent black marker.			
complete a reflection sheet based on his/her artwork.			
listen to and follow instructions.			
work cooperatively in an informal activity-based work environment.			

R.I.C. Publications/Prim-Ed Publishing

White silhouette

This art project was inspired by the theme *People-made disasters*. The impact of humans on the environment was discussed as a topic. Throughout the topic, different civilisations were examined. Ancient nomadic existence was compared with modern civilisation. Salinity problems caused by human interaction with the environment was a focus. (The art strategy of making a white silhouette could be used for any theme.)

Two-lesson project

Discussion points

A colour wheel showing primary, secondary and tertiary colours, and stimulus pictures of saltpans created by removal of vegetation, will enhance meaningful discussion.

- What is 'salinity'? (salty/salt-like)
- What happens to the earth's environment when salinity in the soil is too high? (living things die; vegetation dies causing a chain reaction; animals die etc.)
- What causes high salinity in the soil? (removal of vegetation which keeps salinity to balanced levels)
- What can we do to help overcome the problem of high salinity in the soil? (reduce the amount of vegetation clearing; replant vegetation etc.)

The less humans interact with the environment, the less destruction is caused.

- What is a silhouette? (a dark image outlined against a lighter background)
- Which colours are warm colours? Using the colour wheel (p. vii), discuss primary, secondary and tertiary warm colours.
- Which colours are cool colours? Using the colour wheel (p. vii), discuss primary, secondary and tertiary cool colours.

Lesson one

Materials

- 2 sheets A3 cartridge paper per child
- chalk pastels
- lead pencil
- scissors
- polystyrene (small blocks)
- hot glue gun
- newspaper to protect workspace
- card for mounting
- craft glue for mounting

Method

1. Following discussion about high salinity in the soil and its causes, and warm and cool colours and silhouettes, students use chalk pastels on their sides to colour background in stripes. (Cool colours for the sky and warm colours for the land.) Students use one sheet of A3 cartridge paper in portrait position.

2. Using lead pencil, students draw a tree outline onto second sheet of A3 cartridge paper.

3. Using scissors, carefully cut out tree shape.

4. Using hot glue gun, glue polystyrene blocks onto the back of tree trunk and one small block onto the back of each main branch.

5. Hot glue blocks to the background.

⭐ 6. Enlist adult help to mount work onto coloured card.

Lesson two

Materials

- reflection and assessment photocopies
- lead pencil
- coloured pencils

Method

1. Students complete reflection activity.

2. Teacher completes assessment record.

White silhouette

R.I.C. Publications/Prim-Ed Publishing

White silhouette
Reflections

1. High salinity is an environmental problem. Explain what causes high salinity and its negative consequences.

_____

_____

_____

2. What can be done to try to overcome the problem of high salinity in the soil?

_____

_____

_____

3. Which part of this activity did you enjoy most? Give a reason for your answer.

_____

_____

_____

4. List the tools and materials you used to make this art piece.

_____

_____

5. List four warm colours.

_____

6. List four cool colours.

_____

7. A silhouette is usually dark. Using lead pencil, draw a picture with a dark silhouette. Colour your drawing with pencils. Choose warm colours for the background.

R.I.C. Publications/Prim-Ed Publishing

White silhouette
Task assessment

Activity objectives

Arts ideas: *Creates artworks to express ideas.*
Arts skills and processes: *Uses a range of visual arts skills, techniques, procedures, practices and technologies.*
Arts responses: *Uses an aesthetic understanding to acknowledge, reflect on and assess the arts.*
Arts in society: *Demonstrates an understanding of the part that the arts play in society.*

Task

The students were instructed to make a white silhouette picture using a range of
skills, techniques, mediums and materials.

Assessment key			
✔ **yes** *(has demonstrated achievement of this criterion)*			
✘ **no** *(has not demonstrated achievement of this criterion)*			
● **inconsistent** *(some evidence of achievement has been shown)*			
Criterion			
The student is able to:	✔	✘	●
participate in discussion about high salinity in the soil, warm and cool colours and silhouettes.			
colour warm and cool colour stripes using chalk pastels.			
draw a tree using lead pencil.			
cut accurately using scissors.			
use a hot glue gun and polystyrene blocks to fasten picture to background for a 3-D effect.			
complete a reflection sheet based on his/her artwork.			
listen to and follow instructions.			
work cooperatively in an informal activity-based work environment.			

Primary art **97**

Watercolour masterpiece

This art piece is simple and effective. Any picture/photo may be used, so the level of difficulty may be adjusted by the artist. The purpose of this activity is to develop skills in using watercolour pencils; however, it may also be completed in black and white, using lead pencil.

The fish picture in the example was located on an old calendar. The discussion questions are not based on content as each student will focus on his/her own photo/picture. Photos/pictures may be found in magazines, old calendars, catalogues etc.

Three-lesson project

Discussion points

- What colours can you see in your photo/picture? (Bear in mind the coloured pencil choices available.)
- Are there definite lines in your photo/picture or is there a blurred effect?
- Do the colours blend together or are they in sections?
- Is the background textured or plain?
- Is the background multicoloured?
- Which part of the photo/picture should you start drawing first? (the foreground of the photo/picture if there is depth in the picture: this is the main feature of the photo/picture.)

Lesson one

Materials

- A3 cartridge paper
- selected photo/picture
- glue stick
- lead pencil/eraser
- ruler
- scissors
- paintbrush (fine)
- watercolour pencils
- water containers
- newspaper to protect workspace

Method

1. Following discussion focusing on characteristics of photo/picture, students decide which half of the picture is to be drawn and coloured using watercolour pencils. (The half chosen may be a vertical or horizontal half.)
2. Measure halfway and rule a line across picture.
3. Using scissors, cut picture along the measured line.
4. Set aside half of picture to be drawn and coloured.
5. Using glue stick, glue remaining half of picture onto A3 cartridge paper, allowing room to complete drawing and colouring of picture.
6. Using lead pencil, lightly draw the missing half of the picture.
7. When satisfied with drawing, add colour with watercolour pencils.

Lesson two

Materials

- artwork in progress
- equipment required to complete Lesson one
- water containers
- paintbrush (fine)
- newspaper to protect workspace
- coloured card for mounting
- craft glue for mounting
- scissors or slide paper cutter

Method

1. Using watercolour pencils, complete adding colour to drawing.
2. Using fine paintbrush and water, blend colours where desired. Set aside to dry.
★ 3. Enlist adult help to trim and mount artwork onto coloured card.

Lesson three

Materials

- reflection and assessment photocopies
- lead pencil
- coloured pencils

Method

1. Students complete reflection activity.
2. Teacher completes assessment record.

Watercolour masterpiece
Reflections

1. Which part of this activity did you enjoy most? Give a reason for your answer.

_____

_____

2. Describe the photo/picture you completed.

_____

_____

3. Which part of this activity did you find most challenging? Give a reason for your answer.

_____

_____

_____

4. This watercolour blending technique could be used to enhance the colour of many drawings. Describe another drawing which could be enhanced by this technique.

_____

_____

5. Draw and colour your design/picture from Question 4, adding colour with coloured pencils.

6. Using lead pencil, design a symmetrical pattern which could be reflected by drawing the other half.

Watercolour masterpiece
Task assessment

Activity objectives

Arts ideas: *Creates artworks to express ideas.*

Arts skills and processes: *Uses a range of visual arts skills, techniques, procedures, practices and technologies.*

Arts responses: *Uses an aesthetic understanding to acknowledge, reflect on and assess the arts.*

Arts in society: *Demonstrates an understanding of the part that the arts play in society.*

Task

The students were instructed to complete a photo/picture by drawing and colouring
using a range of skills, techniques, mediums and materials.

Assessment key			
✔ **yes** *(has demonstrated achievement of this criterion)*			
✘ **no** *(has not demonstrated achievement of this criterion)*			
● **inconsistent** *(some evidence of achievement has been shown)*			
Criterion			
The student is able to:	✔	✘	●
participate in discussion about characteristics of selected photo/picture.			
measure and rule a line to halve a photo/picture.			
cut accurately with scissors.			
complete the picture by drawing the missing half.			
add colour to the picture using watercolour pencils.			
blend colours using water and fine brush.			
complete a reflection sheet based on his/her artwork.			
listen to and follow instructions.			
work cooperatively in an informal activity-based work environment.			

CD cover

This project was inspired by the theme *Music*. The students had been studying different types of music, including popular music and music currently being given airplay on the radio. The number one hits over a given period of time are often brought out on a CD. The students were asked to make up a title and design a cover for a collection of such hits. The cover could advertise hits over a year or a decade. The example shown was coloured using fluorescent oil pastels.

Two-lesson project

Discussion points

- Do you own a CD which is a collection of popular songs?
- What is the title of the CD? (Answers will vary.)
- It is important for the title and cover of a CD to have an impact for advertising. People will then remember the title when they go to the shops to purchase it, or notice it while they are browsing.
- What could you title a CD which is a collection of popular songs? List suggestions on the board.
- When you look at a range of CDs, which covers attract your attention? (Answers will vary; often bright colourful designs attract attention.)
- What sort of design might you have on a CD cover for a collection of popular hits? Discuss suggestions; encourage justification for ideas.

Lesson one

Materials

- *photocopy paper (12.5 cm x 12 cm)*
- *cartridge paper (12.5 cm x 12 cm)*
- *lead pencil*
- *colouring mediums:* ~ *watercolour pencils*
  - ~ *marker pens*
  - ~ *oil pastels*
  - ~ *wax crayons*
  - ~ *glitter glue*
- *thick black marker*
- *fine black marker*
- *plastic CD cases to display work*
- *newspaper to protect workspace*

Method

1. Following discussion about popular CD music collections, titles, advertising and eye-catching designs, students use lead pencil to design a CD cover on photocopy paper for a collection of popular hits.

2. When satisfied with design, students use lead pencil to transfer design to cartridge paper.

3. If desired, use black markers to enhance detail. If watercolour pencils are to be used, only permanent (colourfast) markers should be used.

4. Using available colouring mediums, add colour to design.

5. Display finished works inside plastic CD cases.

Lesson two

Materials

- *reflection and assessment photocopies*
- *lead pencil*
- *coloured pencils*

Method

1. Students complete reflection activity.

2. Teacher completes assessment record.

CD cover

R.I.C. Publications/Prim-Ed Publishing

CD cover
Reflections

1. List the tools, mediums and materials you used to make your CD cover.

_____

_____

_____

2. Why is it important for a CD cover to be eye-catching?

_____

_____

3. Which part of this activity did you enjoy most? Give a reason for your answer.

_____

_____

_____

4. Were you pleased with your completed CD cover? | Yes | No |
   Give a reason for your answer.

_____

_____

_____

5. Using lead pencil, design a CD cover for your favourite pop star/group. Colour your design using pencils.

   My favourite pop star/group is

   _____

   _____

   _____

R.I.C. Publications/Prim-Ed Publishing

CD cover
Task assessment

Activity objectives
Arts ideas: *Creates artworks to express ideas.*
Arts skills and processes: *Uses a range of visual arts skills, techniques, procedures, practices and technologies.*
Arts responses: *Uses an aesthetic understanding to acknowledge, reflect on and assess the arts.*
Arts in society: *Demonstrates an understanding of the part that the arts play in society.*

Task
The students were instructed to make a CD cover using a range of skills,
techniques, mediums and materials.

Assessment key		
✔ **yes** *(has demonstrated achievement of this criterion)*		
✗ **no** *(has not demonstrated achievement of this criterion)*		
● **inconsistent** *(some evidence of achievement has been shown)*		
Criterion		
The student is able to:	✔	✗ ●
participate in class discussion about CD covers and advertising.		
choose a title for a CD which is a collection of popular songs over a period of time.		
draw a plan for a CD cover design.		
transfer plan onto cartridge paper.		
colour design using a range of available mediums.		
complete a reflection sheet based on his/her artwork.		
listen to and follow instructions.		
work cooperatively in an informal activity-based work environment.		

Ceramic tile design

This art project was inspired by the maths activity *Symmetry*. The students investigated/experimented by drawing symmetrical designs. At first the designs started as simple and uncomplicated, but they soon developed into complex, intricate and interesting designs.

Three-lesson project

Discussion points

- What is symmetry? (when corresponding opposite sides are identical; therefore a reflection)

A line of symmetry is a line which is central to reflecting sides.

- How can you determine if something is symmetrical, or has a line of symmetry? (Demonstrate symmetrical shapes by drawing shapes on the board and asking students to come out and draw a line of symmetry.)
- Can you name some things/objects which may be symmetrical? (a person; a sheet of paper; a noticeboard; a glass, a wedding ring etc.)
- Can you see things in the classroom which are symmetrical? (Answers will vary.)

Decorative wall and floor tiles often have symmetrical designs as a feature. Tile painting is an ancient art. This design could be used as a feature floor or wall tile.

Lesson one

Materials

- photocopy paper (16 cm x 16 cm)
- lead pencil
- ruler
- thick black marker
- cartridge paper (32 cm x 32 cm)
- newspaper to protect workspace
- example master to show students (page 136)

Method

1. Following maths activities where students have drawn and investigated symmetrical design, students fold photocopy paper square in half diagonally.
2. Using lead pencil, draw a design on one half.
3. Trace using thick black marker.
4. Trace design onto the other half of the paper using black marker.
5. Using this design as the master, trace the design four times onto square cartridge paper. Ensure bottom corner of design is always on the centre of the page.

Lesson two

Materials

- artwork in progress
- thick black marker
- acrylic paint (variety of colours)
- polystyrene trays (for paint)
- paintbrush (fine)
- newspaper to protect workspace

Method

1. Using thick black marker, complete tracing tile design onto cartridge paper.
2. Using fine paintbrush and acrylic paint, paint 'ceramic tile' design. Set aside to dry.

Lesson three

Materials

- artwork in progress
- acrylic paint (variety of colours)
- polystyrene trays (for paint)
- paintbrush (fine)
- coloured card for mounting
- craft glue for mounting
- reflection and assessment photocopies
- lead pencil
- coloured pencils

Method

1. Complete painting 'ceramic tile' design. Set aside to dry.
★ 2. Enlist adult help to mount completed designs onto coloured card.
3. Students complete reflection activity.
4. Teacher completes assessment record.

Ceramic tile design

Ceramic tile design
Reflections

1. List five tools, mediums and materials you used to make your ceramic tile design.

   _____

   _____

2. What does 'symmetrical' mean?

   _____

   _____

3. Which part of this activity did you enjoy most? Give a reason for your answer.

   _____

   _____

   _____

4. Which part of this activity did you find most challenging?

   _____

   _____

5. Were you satisfied with the finished tile design? | Yes | No |
   Give a reason for your answer.

   _____

   _____

6. Ceramic tiles are used to cover floors, benchtops etc. Sometimes they are used as a decorative feature. Draw a design of your choice which you would like to display in your home. Colour your design with pencils.

R.I.C. Publications/Prim-Ed Publishing

Ceramic tile design
Task assessment

Activity objectives
Arts ideas: *Creates artworks to express ideas.*
Arts skills and processes: *Uses a range of visual arts skills, techniques, procedures, practices and technologies.*
Arts responses: *Uses an aesthetic understanding to acknowledge, reflect on and assess the arts.*
Arts in society: *Demonstrates an understanding of the part that the arts play in society.*

Task
The students were instructed to draw and colour a symmetrical design using a range of
skills, techniques, mediums and materials.

Assessment key			
✔ **yes** (has demonstrated achievement of this criterion)			
✘ **no** (has not demonstrated achievement of this criterion)			
● **inconsistent** (some evidence of achievement has been shown)			
Criterion			
The student is able to:	✔	✘	●
participate in discussion about symmetry, symmetrical designs and ceramic tiles.			
draw a symmetrical design.			
trace symmetrical design four times to make a square design.			
add colour to design using paint and a fine brush.			
complete a reflection sheet based on his/her artwork.			
listen to and follow instructions.			
work cooperatively in an informal activity based work environment.			

Word designs

This lesson was inspired by an interest in comics shown by the students during a viewing activity comparing forms of writing. Oil pastels were used to colour this art project; however, a range of colouring mediums would be suitable. In weeks prior to the lesson, students were encouraged to bring in comics.

Two-lesson project

Discussion points

In comics, the writer conveys actions, sounds and happenings by using words such as 'crash', 'zap' and 'bang'. These words may be nouns or verbs, depending on the context in which they are used.

nouns: *naming words*
verbs: *doing/action words*
adjectives: *words which describe nouns*

Superhero comics use such words to emphasise the meaning of the text and pictures.

- What words have you noticed which convey meaning in comics? (Answers will vary depending on the comic examples students bring in.)
- Discuss the use of sharp shapes to convey loud noises. Curved shapes tend to convey a quieter message.

Lesson one

Materials

- recycled photocopy paper 3 x A4 per child
- cartridge paper 3 x A4 per child
- lead pencil
- thick black marker
- oil pastels – fluorescent
- glue stick
- card for mounting
- newspaper to protect workspace
- scissors

Method

1. Following discussion about the use of nouns and verbs to add meaning to text in comics, students choose three words which add meaning to the text in comics.
2. Using lead pencil, students experiment with letter shapes to write words on A4 photocopy paper.
3. Draw surrounding borders, which may be coloured.
4. When satisfied with results, trace over design using black marker.
5. Trace designs onto A4 cartridge paper.
6. Colour word designs using fluorescent oil pastels. Emphasise strong, solid colour.
7. Using scissors, cut out designs.
8. Arrange word designs on A3 black card.
9. Using glue stick, attach word designs in position.

Lesson two

Materials

- reflection and assessment photocopies
- lead pencil
- coloured pencils

Method

1. Students complete reflection activity.
2. Teacher completes assessment record.

R.I.C. Publications/Prim-Ed Publishing

Word designs

Reflections

1. Which part of this activity did you enjoy most? Give a reason for your answer.

_____

_____

_____

2. Which part of this activity was most challenging? Give a reason for your answer.

_____

_____

3. Make a list of materials and a series of instructions for someone else to follow to make the word designs project.

_____

_____

_____

_____

_____

_____

4. Using lead pencil, draw a name design which could be used to decorate a coffee mug. Colour your design using pencils.

R.I.C. Publications/Prim-Ed Publishing

Word designs
Task assessment

Activity objectives

Arts ideas: *Creates artworks to express ideas.*

Arts skills and processes: *Uses a range of visual arts skills, techniques, procedures, practices and technologies.*

Arts responses: *Uses an aesthetic understanding to acknowledge, reflect on and assess the arts.*

Arts in society: *Demonstrates an understanding of the part that the arts play in society.*

Task

The students were instructed to draw word designs using a range of skills, techniques and materials.

Assessment key			
✔ **yes** *(has demonstrated achievement of this criterion)*			
✗ **no** *(has not demonstrated achievement of this criterion)*			
● **inconsistent** *(some evidence of achievement has been shown)*			
Criterion			
The student is able to:	✔	✗	●
participate in discussion about words used to enhance the meaning of the text in comics.			
draw a plan for three words which enhance the meaning of the text in comics.			
trace designs onto cartridge paper.			
draw over tracings using black marker.			
demonstrate strong, solid colouring using oil pastels.			
cut accurately using scissors.			
arrange and glue word designs onto black card.			
complete a reflection sheet based on his/her artwork.			
listen to and follow instructions.			
work cooperatively in an informal activity-based work environment.			

Pencil mania collage

This activity was inspired by a print of a painting a student brought to school as the focus of an art review. The painting was by John Brack, titled *The battle*. The battle represented was the Battle of Waterloo, fought in 1815. The English, French and Prussian armies were involved. Brack painted armies made up of thousands of pencils, representing soldiers.

A focus was placed on recycling. Discarded strips of coloured card were used to create an attractive art piece. The students had been exposed to the different methods of recycling available to reduce wastage of precious natural resources. Accurate measuring is necessary to make the feature pencils in this art piece; therefore, maths work on measurement is incorporated.

Two-lesson project

Discussion points

A picture of a colour wheel is essential to inspire meaningful discussion.

★ *Before the lesson enlist adult help to mount black card onto coloured card background.*

- What was the feature of John Brack's painting *The battle*? (coloured pencils representing soldiers)
- Coloured pencils are bright and colourful. In a pack of twelve coloured pencils, which colours are included? (Answers will vary, depending on the make of pencils students have brought to school.)
- Discuss primary, secondary and tertiary colours.
- What are complementary colours? (colours which are opposite on the colour wheel) Discuss complementary colour combinations. Refer to colour wheel and demonstrate complementary colours.
- What is recycling? (reusing products, especially natural resources, by repeated use or reprocessing)
- What can we do to recycle at home? (ensure that we correctly dispose of recyclable materials; e.g. recycling bins and outlets; wherever possible, return organic materials to the earth; e.g. turning vegetable matter into compost; avoid wasting paper etc.)
- Reusing paper products to make art projects can be a very effective form of recycling.
- Offcuts of coloured card were used to create this pencil collage.

Lesson one

Materials

★ • coloured card offcuts (brown/tan to be cut into 2.5 cm lengths; other colours to be cut into 25 cm lengths)
- black card (50 cm x 38 cm)
- lead pencil
- ruler
- scissors
- glue stick
- card for mounting
- craft glue for mounting
- newspaper to protect workspace

Method

1. Following discussion about John Brack's artwork *The battle*, colours and recycling, and using a glue stick, students glue brown/tan coloured strips approx. 7 mm from the edge of coloured paper. (This forms the base to make pencils.)
2. On the back of coloured paper, measure 1-cm margins to make the pencils.
3. Using scissors, cut carefully along the lines.
4. Cut v shapes to make the colouring end of the pencil.
5. Arrange pencils into a collage.
6. Using glue stick, glue pencils into position.

Lesson two

Materials

- *reflection and assessment photocopies*
- *lead pencil*
- *coloured pencils*

Method

1. Students complete reflection activity.
2. Teacher completes assessment record.

R.I.C. Publications/Prim-Ed Publishing

Pencil mania collage

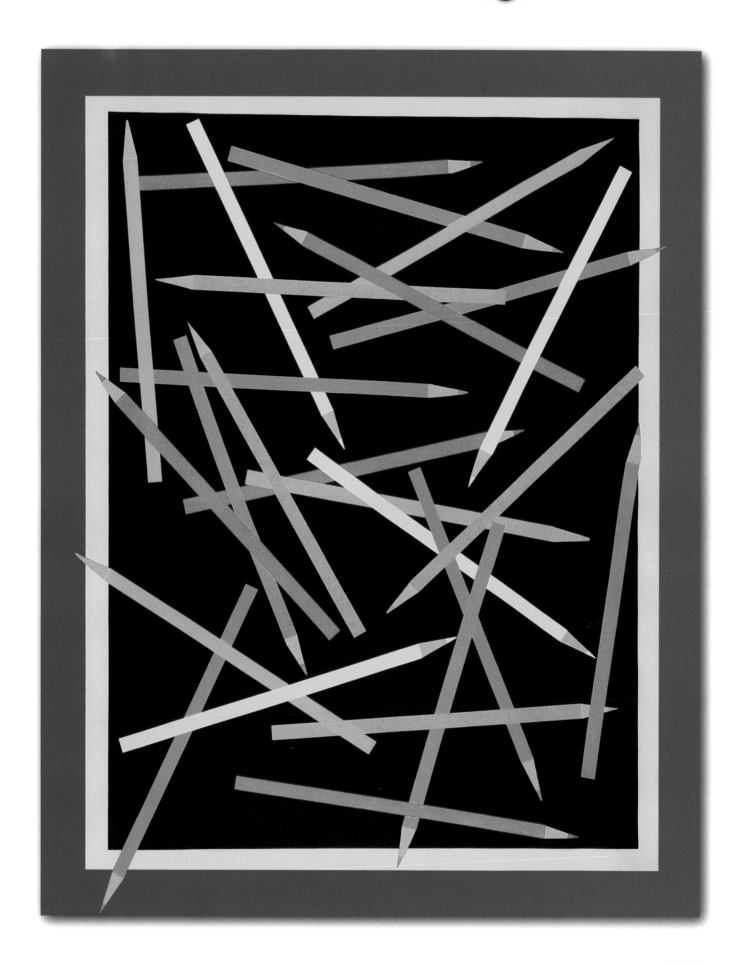

Pencil mania collage
Reflections

1. List five tools, mediums and materials you used to complete your collage.

_____

_____

_____

2. Which part of this activity did you enjoy most? Give a reason for your answer.

_____

_____

3. What are complementary colours? _____

_____

_____

4. List the three pairs of complementary colours.

_____

_____

5. Why is it important to recycle?

_____

_____

_____

_____

_____

_____

_____

_____

_____

6. John Brack's painting, The battle, represented soldiers with pencils. Using lead pencil, design a pencil character. Colour your design with pencils.

Pencil mania collage
Task assessment

Activity objectives

Arts ideas: *Creates artworks to express ideas.*

Arts skills and processes: *Uses a range of visual arts skills, techniques, procedures, practices and technologies.*

Arts responses: *Uses an aesthetic understanding to acknowledge, reflect on and assess the arts.*

Arts in society: *Demonstrates an understanding of the part that the arts play in society.*

Task

The students were instructed to make a pencil collage using a range
of skills, techniques, mediums and materials.

Assessment key			
✔ **yes** (has demonstrated achievement of this criterion)			
✗ **no** (has not demonstrated achievement of this criterion)			
● **inconsistent** (some evidence of achievement has been shown)			
Criterion			
The student is able to:	✔	✗	●
participate in discussion about John Brack's The battle, *colours and recycling.*			
glue coloured strips of paper accurately into position.			
measure 1 cm and rule 1-cm margins accurately.			
cut accurately along lines using scissors.			
arrange and glue pencil shapes in a collage.			
complete a reflection sheet based on his/her artwork.			
listen to and follow instructions.			
work cooperatively in an informal activity-based work environment.			

R.I.C. Publications/Prim-Ed Publishing

Simple self-portrait

This art project was inspired by the theme *Colour*. Cool, warm and complementary colours were the focus. A simple line drawing was photocopied and the students experimented with colour, painting the same drawing with cool, warm and complementary colours.

Three-lesson project

Discussion points

A picture/poster of a colour wheel is essential to inspire meaningful discussion.

- What is a simple line drawing? (a drawing with only the main features included in the detail)
- Which colours are warm colours? (Refer to the colour wheel.)
- Which colours are the cool colours? (Refer to the colour wheel.)
- What are complementary colours? (colours which are directly opposite on the colour wheel)

Lesson one

Materials

- photocopy paper (15 cm x 12 cm) (one sheet per child)
- lead pencil/eraser
- fine black marker

Method

1. Following discussion about simple drawings, warm colours, cool colours and complementary colours, on precut photocopy paper and using lead pencil, students draw a simple drawing of themselves. When satisfied, erase unwanted lines and trace over remaining lines with fine black marker.

★ 2. Enlist adult help to make four photocopies of each student's simple drawing on cartridge paper.

Lesson two

Materials

- artwork in progress (photocopies of simple drawings)
- acrylic paint —primary and secondary colours
- polystyrene trays (for paint)
- paintbrush (fine)
- black and coloured card for mounting
- craft glue for mounting
- newspaper to protect workspace

Method

(One simple drawing will be painted with cool colours; one simple drawing will be painted with warm colours; and two simple drawings will be painted with complementary colours.)

1. Choose warm, cool and complementary colours to paint simple drawings.

2. Using paint and brush, colour simple drawings. Set aside to dry.

★ 3. Enlist adult help to mount pictures onto black and coloured card.

Lesson three

Materials

- reflection and assessment photocopies
- lead pencil
- coloured pencils

Method

1. Students complete reflection activity.

2. Teacher completes assessment record.

Simple self-portrait

Simple self-portrait
Reflections

1. What is a simple drawing? _____

_____

2. List the two warm colours you used to colour your self-portrait.

_____

3. List the two cool colours you used to colour your self-portrait.

_____

4. List the two sets of complementary colours you used to colour your self-portrait.

_____

5. When you experimented with colour, were you satisfied with your results? Give a reason for your answer.

Yes	No

_____

_____

6. Which part of this activity did you find most challenging?

_____

_____

7. Write a set of instructions for someone else to complete this art project. Include a list of materials.

_____

_____

_____

_____

_____

_____

_____

_____

_____

_____

8. Using lead pencil, draw an object, then colour it with pencils in warm, cool or complementary colours. Label your drawing with the category of colours you chose.

Simple self-portrait
Task assessment

Activity objectives

Arts ideas: *Creates artworks to express ideas.*

Arts skills and processes: *Uses a range of visual arts skills, techniques, procedures, practices and technologies.*

Arts responses: *Uses an aesthetic understanding to acknowledge, reflect on and assess the arts.*

Arts in society: *Demonstrates an understanding of the part that the arts play in society.*

Task

The students were instructed to complete a simple self-portrait using
a range of skills and basic materials.

Assessment key			
✔ **yes** (has demonstrated achievement of this criterion)			
✗ **no** (has not demonstrated achievement of this criterion)			
● **inconsistent** (some evidence of achievement has been shown)			
Criterion			
The student is able to:	✔	✗	●
participate in discussion about simple drawings, warm colours, cool colours and complementary colours.			
complete a simple self-portrait.			
paint four copies of the simple drawing using warm, cool and complementary colours.			
complete a reflection sheet based on his/her artwork.			
listen to and follow instructions.			
work cooperatively in an informal activity-based work environment.			

Colourful creatures

This art project was inspired by the theme *Fantasy,* which incorporated several learning areas and involved narrative writing about a Fantasy creature. The students made a symmetrical painting of the main character as a lead-up to writing an adventure story.

Three-lesson project

Discussion points

Stimulus pictures of creatures from books and movies are useful to stimulate meaningful discussion.

- Where are we most likely to see fantasy creatures and monsters? (in movies; read about them in books)

- What effect does it have on us when we see or read about an unreal scary creature? (it stimulates our imagination; it can make us feel frightened even though we know it is not real)

- Why is it important for parents to monitor what young students watch and read? (Young students may not be able to truly believe that the creatures/ monsters aren't real and they could be frightened for a long time. Some students cope better than others with scary images. Introduce the concept of movie ratings.)

- In your imagination, what does your creature look like? (include human-like features ... does it have arms, legs, eyes etc.?)
- How does it move around?
- What colours are on its body?
- What unusual features does it have?
- What does 'symmetrical' mean? (even on both sides; identical; mirror image)

Lesson one ●●

Materials

- A3 cartridge paper
- acrylic paint (variety of fluorescent colours in squeeze bottles)
- polystyrene trays (for paint)
- block sponges
- lead pencil

- coloured pencils
- A4 photocopy paper (for plan)
- newspaper to protect workspace

Method

1. Following discussion, students sponge paint A3 cartridge paper background using a 'pat and lift' motion (no dragging).

   Students may choose two or three weird and wonderful colours for the background, as this is a fantasy picture. Set aside to dry.

2. Teacher demonstrates how to create a creature using instructions in Lesson two. This is a 'paint and smooth' technique.

   Note: If a more defined image is preferred, a fine paintbrush, applying the paint generously, may be used. Bear in mind image won't be as vibrant (less paint).

3. Fold photocopy paper in half lengthwise and, using lead pencil, students draw a plan of half of their creature. Use coloured pencils to show the colours to be used.

Lesson two

Materials

- artwork in progress
- acrylic paint (in squeeze bottles)
- paintbrushes (fine) and polystyrene trays if defined image is preferred
- newspaper to protect workspace
- card for mounting
- craft glue for mounting

Method

1. Fold painted background in half lengthways.

2. Using squeezy bottles, apply paint to represent one half of the creature or paint half of the creature using a fine brush, applying paint generously.

3. Carefully fold page in half, smoothing the page gently.

4. Unfold paper and set aside to dry. (This may take up to 48 hours if paintings are very wet.)

★ 5. Enlist adult help to mount work onto coloured card.

Lesson three

Materials

- artwork in progress
- acrylic paint (black and white)
- polystyrene trays (for paint)
- arbitrary tools (flat-ended pencil, marker, glue stick lid, bamboo skewers)
- paintbrush (fine)
- newspaper to protect workspace
- reflection and assessment photocopies
- coloured pencils
- lead pencil

Method

1. Add detail to artwork by printing with arbitrary tools and brush painting. (eyes – flat end of marker and a lead pencil; teeth – fine brush; feet, hand, mouth and nostril – flat end of kebab skewer) Set aside to dry.

2. Students complete reflection activity.

2. Teacher completes assessment record.

R.I.C. Publications/Prim-Ed Publishing

Colourful creatures

Colourful creatures
Reflections

1. List the tools and materials you used for this project.

_____

_____

_____

2. Which part of the project did you enjoy the most? Give a reason for your answer.

_____

_____

_____

3. Did you achieve the result your were aiming for on your plan? Include any changes you made to improve your result next time.

_____

_____

_____

_____

4. What does 'symmetrical' mean?

_____

_____

_____

_____

5. Why is it important for parents to monitor a young child's viewing of scary creature/monster movies?

_____

_____

_____

6. What is the purpose of movie ratings?

_____

_____

_____

7. Using lead pencil, draw another plan for a colourful monster you could make using a 'paint and smooth' technique. Show the colours by using coloured pencils.

R.I.C. Publications/Prim-Ed Publishing

Colourful creatures
Task assessment

Activity objectives

Arts ideas: *Creates artworks to express ideas.*

Arts skills and processes: *Uses a range of visual arts skills, techniques, procedures, practices and technologies.*

Arts responses: *Uses an aesthetic understanding to acknowledge, reflect on and assess the arts.*

Arts in society: *Demonstrates an understanding of the part that the arts play in society.*

Task

The students were instructed to make a colourful creature picture using a range of skills and techniques.

Assessment key			
✔ **yes** *(has demonstrated achievement of this criterion)*			
✘ **no** *(has not demonstrated achievement of this criterion)*			
● **inconsistent** *(some evidence of achievement has been shown)*			
Criterion			
The student is able to:	✔	✘	●
participate in class discussion about fantasy and colourful creatures.			
demonstrate sponge painting using a 'pat and lift' motion.			
draw a plan of half a monster, bearing in mind a line of symmetry.			
paint half a creature onto folded background using squeeze bottles of paint or brush and acrylic paint.			
fold the picture in half and gently smooth the paint to make a symmetrical painting.			
add detail to picture using arbitrary tools and acrylic paint.			
complete a reflection sheet based on his/her artwork.			
listen to and follow instructions.			
work cooperatively in an informal activity-based work environment.			

Primary art **125**

Summer sunset

This lesson was inspired by the theme *Weather*. As part of the theme, the students studied weather throughout the day and the various sky scenes which formed throughout the 24-hour day. The focus of the scene was a summer sunset.

A range of sunset photographs was observed, with an emphasis on the colours and the reflection of the hues on objects/things in a scene. Creating depth in a 2-D picture through simple shading was also a focus.

Two-lesson project

Discussion points

Photographs of various sunsets showing a range of hues will stimulate discussion and activity. The focus of discussion questions may be directed to available photographs and/or draw on the student's own visual experiences.

- Where have you seen an outstanding sunset? (Answers will vary, depending on location.)
- What colours did you notice? Incorporate warm and cool terminology. (Answers will vary.)
- Discuss the reflection of colour on objects in the scene.
- Are the colours distinct or do they blend together?
- How can we add dimension to a 2-D drawing? (shading using slightly curved lines—as shown to create curved bricklaying; shading—as shown to create depth in rocks.)
- Demonstrate drawing curved and varied-length lines to enhance depth using a touch of a darker colour; add highlights to enhance detail as shown in example.

Lesson one

Materials

- *A3 cartridge paper*
- *oil pastels*
- *chalk pastels*
- *newspaper to protect workspace*
- *coloured card to mount work*
- *craft glue for mounting*

Method

1. Following discussion about sunsets, colour and reflection, students draw a scene using one dominant colour of oil pastel.
2. Using oil pastels, draw in main features (in this example, windows, door, brick detail, light shape, rocky ground etc.).
3. Using oil and chalk pastels, add colour to drawing, emphasising shape by drawing curved lines.
4. Shade to add dimension and reflection (in this example, windows, lamp, light rays etc.)

5. Using chalk pastels, gently draw lines of purple and orange across the background. Smudge colours together to form a blended sunset. It is not necessary to colour the whole area with chalk as smudging spreads the colour.

   This lesson will require finishing time. If equipment is kept handy, it may be worked on when other class work is completed early.

★ 6. Enlist adult help to mount work onto coloured card.

Lesson two

Materials

- *reflection and assessment photocopies*
- *lead pencil*
- *coloured pencils*

Method

1. Students complete reflection activity.
2. Teacher completes assessment record.

Summer sunset

R.I.C. Publications/Prim-Ed Publishing

Summer sunset
Reflections

Name: ....   Date: ....

1. Which part of this activity did you enjoy most? Give a reason for your answer.

_____

_____

_____

2. Where is your sunset? (the beach/over the sea, a lighthouse, over the city etc.)

_____

_____

3. Describe how you created depth and shape in your drawing.

_____

_____

4. In the space below, draw two shapes which demonstrate two different drawing techniques which can create depth and shape in a drawing.

5. Were you able to achieve the blended colour effect to create a colourful sunset?

Yes	No

6. Describe the technique you used to achieve this.

_____

_____

_____

R.I.C. Publications/Prim-Ed Publishing

Name: .... **Year:** .... **Date:** ....

Summer sunset
Task assessment

Activity objectives
Arts ideas: *Creates artworks to express ideas.*
Arts skills and processes: *Uses a range of visual arts skills, techniques, procedures, practices and technologies.*
Arts responses: *Uses an aesthetic understanding to acknowledge, reflect on and assess the arts.*
Arts in society: *Demonstrates an understanding of the part that the arts play in society.*

Task
The students were instructed to make a summer sunset picture using a range of skills and techniques, mediums and materials.

Assessment key
✔ **yes** (has demonstrated achievement of this criterion)
✗ **no** (has not demonstrated achievement of this criterion)
● **inconsistent** (some evidence of achievement has been shown)

Criterion			
The student is able to:	✔	✗	●
participate in class discussion about summer sunsets, colours and reflection of colour.			
draw a scene at sunset.			
demonstrate depth using varied-length, straight-line shading.			
demonstrate depth using curved line shading.			
demonstrate shape using curved lines.			
include colour reflection on objects in his/her drawing.			
demonstrate colour blending using chalk pastels.			
complete a reflection sheet based on his/her artwork.			
listen to and follow instructions.			
work cooperatively in an informal activity-based work environment.			

Primary art **129**

Resources

Page 131 – Etched name leaning board

Page 132 – Porthole scene

Page 133 – Butterfly farm

Page 134 – Mermaid/Merman

Page 135 – Terrific tourist T-shirt

Page 136 – Ceramic tile design

Templates should be made from card, such as cereal box/lightweight strawboard. Adults can help to make templates prior to lessons, depending on the age and ability of students and the difficulty of the art project. Instructions for some templates are given, although teachers may design their own or alter sizes to suit.

Be environmentally friendly by using household packaging to make sets of reusable templates.

R.I.C. Publications/Prim-Ed Publishing

Etched name leaning board

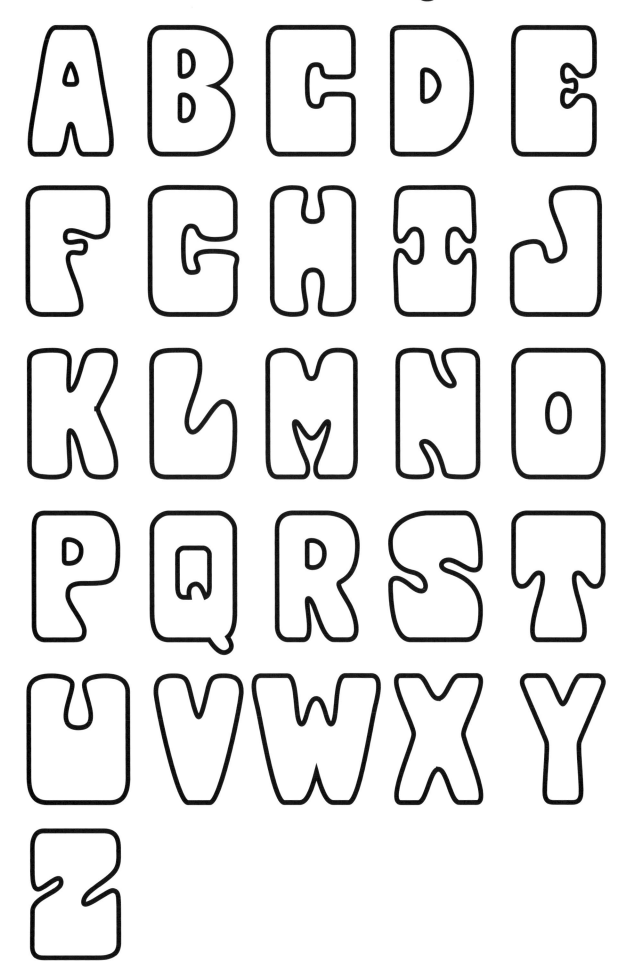

Porthole scene

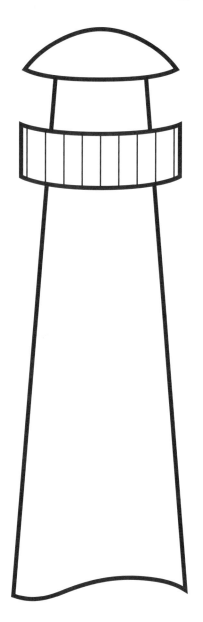

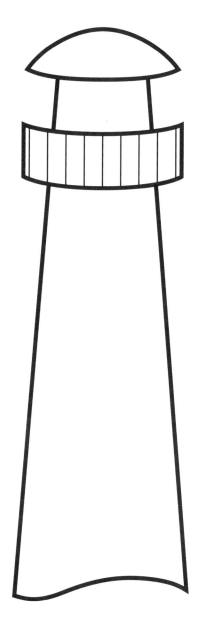

R.I.C. Publications/Prim-Ed Publishing

Butterfly farm

R.I.C. Publications/Prim-Ed Publishing

Mermaid/Merman

Enlarge template to appropriate size.

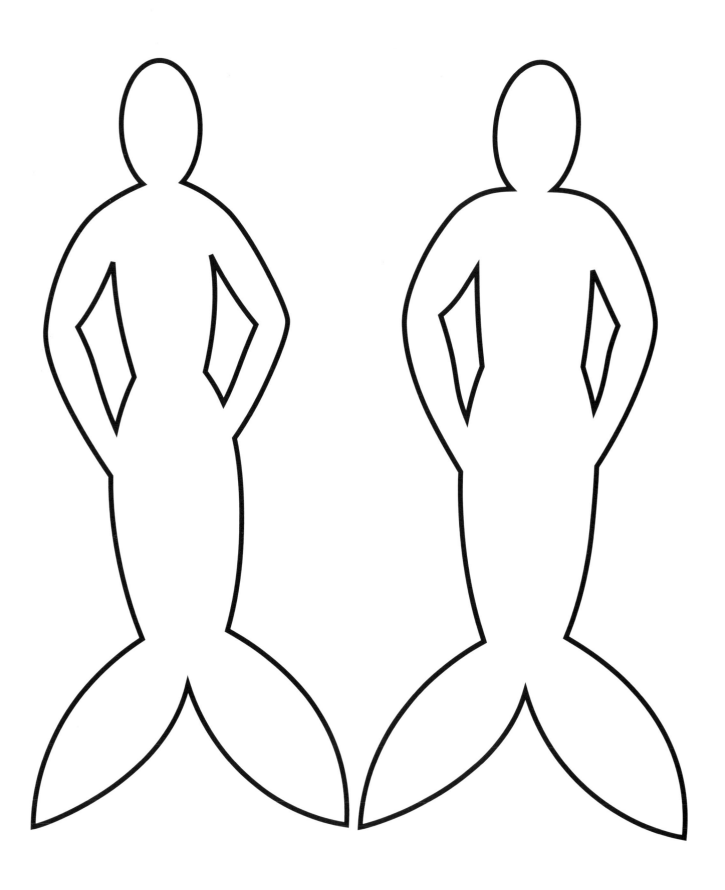

R.I.C. Publications/Prim-Ed Publishing

Terrific tourist T-shirt

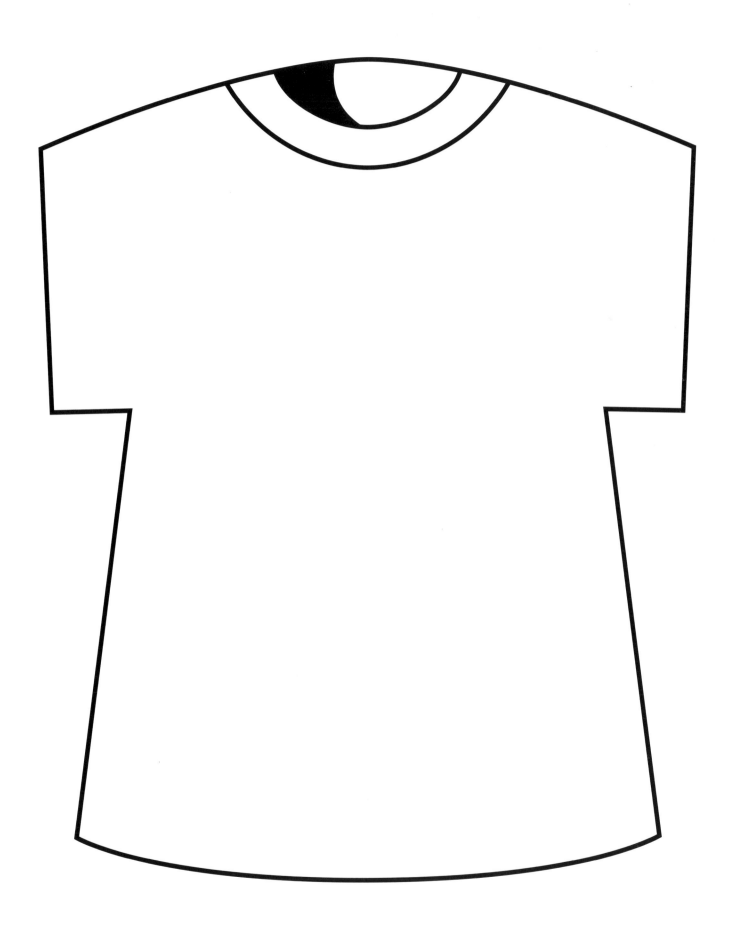

R.I.C. Publications/Prim-Ed Publishing

Ceramic tile design

R.I.C. Publications/Prim-Ed Publishing